JavaScript Creativity

Exploring the Modern Capabilities of JavaScript and HTML5

Shane Hudson

Apress

JavaScript Creativity: Exploring the Modern Capabilities of JavaScript and HTML5

ISBN-13 (pbk): 978-1-4302-5944-2

ISBN-13 (electronic): 978-1-4302-5945-9

Publisher: Heinz Weinheimer
Lead Editor: Louise Corrigan
Technical Reviewer: Keith Cirkel
Editorial Board: Steve Anglin, Mark Beckner, Ewan Buckingham, Gary Cornell, Louise Corrigan, Jim DeWolf, Jonathan Gennick, Jonathan Hassell, Robert Hutchinson, Michelle Lowman, James Markham, Matthew Moodie, Jeff Olson, Jeffrey Pepper, Douglas Pundick, Ben Renow-Clarke, Dominic Shakeshaft, Gwenan Spearing, Matt Wade, Steve Weiss
Coordinating Editors: Christine Ricketts and Mark Powers
Copy Editor: Linda Seifert
Compositor: SPi Global
Indexer: SPi Global
Artist: SPi Global
Cover Designer: Anna Ishchenko

Distributed to the book trade worldwide by Springer Science+Business Media New York, 233 Spring Street, 6th Floor, New York, NY 10013. Phone 1-800-SPRINGER, fax (201) 348-4505, e-mail orders-ny@springer-sbm.com, or visit www.springeronline.com. Apress Media, LLC is a California LLC and the sole member (owner) is Springer Science + Business Media Finance Inc (SSBM Finance Inc). SSBM Finance Inc is a Delaware corporation.

For information on translations, please e-mail rights@apress.com, or visit www.apress.com.

Apress and friends of ED books may be purchased in bulk for academic, corporate, or promotional use. eBook versions and licenses are also available for most titles. For more information, reference our Special Bulk Sales–eBook Licensing web page at www.apress.com/bulk-sales.

Any source code or other supplementary material referenced by the author in this text is available to readers at www.apress.com. For detailed information about how to locate your book's source code, go to www.apress.com/source-code/.

Dedicated to my parents: John and Michelle

Contents at a Glance

Contents

About the Author

Shane Hudson is a web developer with a strong interest in both bleeding edge web technologies and web standards. He has extensive experience with JavaScript, having worked on a range of highly interactive websites and side projects. He also has interest in the fields of artificial intelligence and computer vision. You can contact Shane by email at shane@shanehudson.net or on Twitter @ShaneHudson.

About the Technical Reviewer

Keith Cirkel is a JavaScript Consultant from London, United Kingdom, specializing in writing open source JavaScript libraries and literature. To find out more about his work, visit http://keithcirkel.co.uk, reach him via GitHub at github.com/keithamus, or Twitter at twitter.com/keithamus.

Acknowledgments

It wasn't until I wrote this book that I really understood why every author's acknowledgments say, "This book would not be possible without…." If it were not for these people that helped me throughout the writing process, I would have given up and there would be no book.

I must start by thanking Louise Corrigan, my wonderful editor, for absolutely everything. I originally just casually asked her who I should talk to about writing a book, then just a few months later I had signed my contract. Throughout the process she has encouraged me (there were many times when I wanted to just stop writing) and helped develop the ideas for each chapter. Without Louise, I am certain that this book would be just a figment of my imagination, but instead you are holding it in your hands. Thank you Louise, for believing in me.

Before starting the book, I had no idea what the role of coordinating editor meant. Mark Powers and Christine Ricketts were my two coordinating editors, and they are both incredible people. It took me far longer to write the book than I had expected and yet both Mark and Christine did a great job making sure everything went as smoothly as possible.

The final member of staff from Apress that I owe a great many thanks to is Linda Seifert, who copyedited the entire book. I may have written a book now but I am still a programmer, so Linda was like a magician turning my strings of words into sentences worthy of being published.

I know there were also many other people working behind the scenes on the book, whom I had little contact with. So I would like to say thank you to those people too.

My technical reviewer throughout the book was Keith Cirkel and I truly could not have been luckier. Keith is a great guy and an incredible programmer. He constantly gave me ideas on how to improve not only the code but the flow of the chapters as well. Much of the code was written late at night and he was able to pick up lots of ways to improve the code, rather than just testing that it ran without errors.

Alongside the people working with me on the book, I have some other people that deserve acknowledgement for their varied support with the book. First is Ryan Lamvohee, a programmer from Australia. I've never met Ryan in person, but he was the first programmer I ever got to know online and has supported me ever since. It was Ryan's interest in programming computers to make music that I learned much of what I wrote in Chapter 5 about music theory in JavaScript. Ryan also helped a great deal with the beginning of the book, developing ideas for the example projects.

I of course need to thank Jeremy Keith for writing the foreword of this book. I really wanted Jeremy to write it, but I didn't expect him to do so! He is an incredible writer, deeply thoughtful, and a true asset to the web. When I asked him for a title to put along side his name, I expected it to be to do with Clearleft (where he was one of the founders). Instead he asked for "Ambassador to the Web." If it were any one else, I would be wary of that title—but Jeremy really does deserve it.

Stuart Memo was another inspiration for Chapter 5, having given a brilliant talk titled "JavaScript is the new Punk Rock" that I highly recommend you watch. Stuart has also done a great many other interesting things with the Web Audio API so take a look at his website: www.stuartmemo.com. Originally, I was going to write my own 3D music visualization but no matter what I did, I could not (at least in the time I had) do better than the one Steven Wittens had already explained in a lot of detail. So I was very thankful when Steven gave me his permission to use his visualization in the book. I highly recommend you read his article explaining the math behind the visualization, as well as the other articles on Steven's incredible website: www.acko.net.

Both Matt Diamond and Keith Norman were also very helpful to the development of the book. Matt wrote the Recorder.js script that allows recording of the Web Audio API nodes and he helped with some problems I had using it. Keith Norman wrote the base code for the Web RTC code that I used in Chapter 8 and helped to review my code.

Throughout the book I had a lot of support from my family and friends, especially of course my parents (who I dedicated to book to). Everybody was thrilled for me and tried to help keep me enthused. I would like to give special thanks to everybody in the University of Kent's School of Computing and Plymouth Marine Laboratory's Remote Sensing Department for their consistent support. I would also like to thank my housemates, Edd Greer and Silvana Mallor Hoya, who both put up with me working all hours of the day and helped me see the book to its end. There are so many other people that I wish I could give acknowledgement to but my final thank you goes to Sam Hutchings, a friend of mine that I consider to be a wordsmith. He helped with some of the phrasing and was another person who helped my enthusiasm without which I would not have finished writing this book. And lastly, thank you to everybody on Twitter that put up with all my moaning throughout the writing process!

Foreword

It seems like the World Wide Web is forever playing catch-up. Back in the '90s, the web was competing with CD-ROMs and coming up short—at least in terms of what could be technically accomplished. CD-ROMs offered richer interactivity, better visuals, and the possibility of using audio. But in the long run, that didn't matter. CD-ROMs just couldn't compete with the sheer vastness of the world wide web.

Later on, Macromedia (and later, Adobe) Flash went toe-to-toe with the web. Once again, it seemed like the web couldn't match its competitor for animation, audio, and video. And yet, once again, the web outlasted its flashier counterpart.

More recently, we've seen a rerun of this same story in the world of mobile. Compared to native apps, the web just doesn't appear to offer the same level of rich interactivity. But even here, I suspect that the web will still be stronger than ever long after the craze for native apps has faded away.

Each one of these proprietary technologies—CD-ROMs, Flash, native apps—could be interpreted as a threat to the open web, but I prefer to see them as the web's R'n'D department. There'll always be some competing technology that superficially appears to be gunning for the web's dominance. In reality, these technologies demonstrate what kind of features web developers are looking for from browsers and standards bodies. If it weren't for Flash, would we even have CSS animations? If it weren't for native apps, would there be so much work put into providing access to device APIs?

The web will always be lagging behind some other technology and that's okay. Over time, the web's feature set grows and grows, all the while maintaining backward-compatibility (something sorely missing from those competing technologies). The growth of the web's feature-set might sometimes appear to be painfully slow, but it's worth taking a step back every now and then to see how far we've come.

This book is like a snapshot of the cutting edge of what's possible in web browsers today. The progress we've made might surprise you. It certainly surprised me. I'm somewhat flabbergasted by how much we can accomplish now with audio, video, and animations. And there's no better person than Shane to do the flabbergasting. He's like the Doogie Howser of web development. (Ask your parents.)

So settle in for a wild ride. Shane Hudson is going to take you to the edge.

—Jeremy Keith
Ambassador to the Web

CHAPTER 1

■ ■ ■

Introduction

In this book, we will go on a journey down the rabbit hole of HTML5 and modern JavaScript, exploring a lot of different subjects as we go. We will start with canvas, which many of you will already be familiar with, and use it for two examples: a flocking animation and a coloring book app. Each chapter shows you how each topic can be used in the real world; how HTML5 and JavaScript can be used together to create useful applications and not just for making games or cool demos (although it will also help with those too). The book is split into three main projects, with some additional examples along the way. Every example (especially the main projects) aims to be a good starting point from which to play around and explore, because as useful as books are with their structured approach to learning, there is nothing better than just diving into the code yourself.

After canvas we will, in Chapter 3, delve into using audio and video on the web; this chapter primarily focuses on the Web Audio API, as well as both the audio and video HTML elements. The API is extremely powerful, so the chapter is only a brief introduction and is mostly about visualization of audio, which ties in nicely with Chapter 2, which uses canvas as the base for the graphics. We then move onto 3D graphics, exploring the basics of 3D on the web. I've decided to use the popular library Three.js for handling the WebGL, since pure WebGL "shader code" is rather complicated and very similar to the C language. There are multiple examples along the way in Chapter 4 but the main example is a 3D node graph that shows relationships between films and actors/actresses. I chose this example because data visualization is an extremely useful technique and one of the areas that I have a strong interest in, it is also a good way to show what these new technologies have allowed us to do natively on the web.

In Chapter 5, we will be going on a bit of a tangent into the realm of music theory because the first main project is going to be a music player that includes 3D visualization and music creation; this will nicely tie together all the chapters up until this point. The chapter builds heavily on the introduction to the Web Audio API in Chapter 3, however instead of visualization it generates sound (which can hopefully be used as a starting point for music). Of course, as with all the chapters, it is only a peek into a large discipline so I aim for it to be a good starting point rather than a comprehensive guide. The music theory aspect of Chapter 3 is one of the reasons why this book is called *JavaScript Creativity*; it is not about design or even focused on what you can do with canvas—it is about the creativity of applying web technologies to more than just a blog or an online store.

The music player project is put together in Chapter 6. I use Backbone as a way to bind together all the data, although you are welcome to convert it and instead use something else such as Ember or even just ES6.

The next project is comprised of Chapters 7 and 8. The project is a video chat application using WebRTC and Node.js. Chapter 7 will be a brief introduction to using Node.js for a text-based chat room and Chapter 8 will be a fairly in-depth look into how WebRTC works and how to use it. This will be a useful chapter for many because video chat is a common project that people want to make, especially within some businesses. The project also provides the introduction to getUserMedia that will be needed for the final project (Chapters 9 and 10) involving motion and object detection using the webcam.

Object detection is not a field that is particularly common within the web industry, but it has always been an interest of mine and we now have native capabilities for accessing the webcam (and even more complex techniques such as Web Workers, although I will not be using them in this book) so it makes sense that I would be doing computer vision on the web! The final project, involving object detection, is possibly less useful than the others but more interesting and hopefully it will be the perfect starting place for anybody interested in the subject as well as showing how powerful the web platform really is. The majority of computer vision algorithms are math based and confusing, so I've gone for naïve algorithms (simple to understand but have many edge cases that are not catered for), as well as using a library for more advanced object detection so that you can have an introduction without being bombarded with academia.

The final project ties together all the chapters. It is a real time multi-user, computer-generated, gesture-controlled musical band. This is an ambitious project and is by no means perfect. It is a great way to practice everything in the book and is (I hope) a fun and unique project. The music generated will not be great, it will probably lag and not sound very good but I think it will be the perfect end to the book; after all, my main purpose of the book is to get you involved with projects that you may have not even thought about before!

What You Need to Know

Now that you know the journey we will be going on with this book, it is important to be able to start it. The book is being sold as requiring a working knowledge of JavaScript. This is quite true, but it is written in such a way that, although some of the code is quite complicated, it should be fairly accessible to anybody with some programming background.

■ **Note**   This chapter will focus on the basics, namely debugging, so most of you will probably want to continue to chapter 2 for the introduction to canvas.

CSS

I just wanted to say that knowledge of CSS is expected, but not particularly needed. I use CSS in some chapters to style parts of a page but I tend to focus on the code throughout the book so nothing is polished design-wise and CSS use is minimal. You can get by fine without knowing any, but just be aware that if I do use some it will not be explained.

Debugging

Debugging is, at least in my opinion, a programmer's best skill because quite often code will not work as expected (especially across browsers) and even if it does it can always be improved. Most of the code in this book relies on cutting-edge technologies and many specs have changed even while I wrote the book—so if anything doesn't work, then it could be due to the implementation having changed since I wrote it or the browser you are using doesn't support it.

Browser Compatibility

The first thing to check is whether your browser is compatible with the features being used. This is something you should already be familiar with if you've ever used any modern technologies in production because many users still use browsers that do not support it. Of course, in this case you should be writing code in a "progressive enhancement" way so that the modern browsers get the modern features but it does not break the older browsers. However, throughout this book (because it is about cutting-edge technologies and features) I do not support older browsers and quite often at the time of writing the code only works in one or two browsers. Unless otherwise stated, I test all the code using Google Chrome 31. Most of it should also work in Mozilla Firefox.

The browsers change rapidly these days, in fact while I was writing the book Chrome forked Webkit into Blink and it has already affected specifications because they no longer always agree to go the same route. So what we need is a way to know when different versions of browsers change the implementation. Unfortunately, apart from looking through the change logs or bug tracker, there is no way to know if something has been changed. Luckily, we do know when features are added (which is enough for the majority of cases) due to two open source projects: `www.html5please.com` and `www.caniuse.com`. HTML5 Please is used to easily know if using a feature in production is recommended, and Can I Use is used to know in which browsers a feature is supported.

JavaScript Console

Every browser has different developer tools, some are similar and some quite different but one similarity that all browsers have is the JavaScript Console. This is where all errors are logged, but it is often much more powerful than just an error log. I discuss it from a Google Chrome viewpoint, but most browsers have very similar commands.

Access to variables

Often you will want to know a variable's value so that you can verify it is what you would expect or even just to learn how the data is structured (especially for objects). To do this, simply type the name of the variable into the JavaScript console and the value will be output below the name, this works for all types including objects and arrays. There are a few ways to access the variables via the console:

- After the code has run – If you are only interested in the final outcome, just do as I explained above and type the variable name.

- Breakpoint - I will discuss breakpoints in more detail shortly but as with debuggers in many other languages, you are able to add a breakpoint that allows you to examine the variables at the point that the code at the breakpoint is executed.

- Debugger Statements - You can manually add breakpoints in your code by writing `debugger;` in your code. It is generally easier to use breakpoints, but worth knowing about the debugger statement.

- Inside the code – You can log to the console from within the code. It is usually easier to use breakpoints but if you wish to you can log by writing `console.log('foo');` within the code.

- As a table – This is currently only available in Google Chrome and Firebug but it is a very useful way to view arrays as tabular data where each index is a row. By running `console.table(array);` from either within the code or within the console (I would recommend straight from console, during a breakpoint, since it is not compatible with other browsers).

Prompt

The area that you are able to type into within the console is known as the prompt, since it is used in much the same way as a shell (command line) prompt is used. This is very useful for accessing the console API, such as `console.log` and `console.table`. But it is also far more powerful, since it can evaluate expressions. These could be as basic as simple calculation (the answer gets outputted straight away) or something more specific to the page you're on such as modifying the DOM. In fact, you can write any JavaScript within the prompt, which makes it an invaluable tool for debugging since you can for example take a function that is not working as you would expect it to and modify it without affecting the rest of the script.

Sources

As with the console, most JavaScript debugging tools (within browsers and/or plugins) have a way to view the source code - which makes sense since you usually need to see the code to understand and debug it – but it is not just read-only. These tools allow you to manipulate and debug the code line by line. In Google Chrome, it is found under the 'Sources' tab, although most of the features are available in most other tools too.

Live editing

Sometimes you want to be able to write a line or code or test out a function, that is what the prompt is for, but sometimes you want to change the code itself a variety of times and to see how it does affect the rest of the codebase. Rather than using the prompt or repeatedly saving in your text editor, you can go into the source tab and directly edit the code. This will run it in a new instance of the JavaScript Virtual Machine so that you can test and debug all you need to without overwriting the original file (which would then need to be refreshed, and you may lose useful code et cetera).

Breakpoints

You are likely already familiar with basic breakpoints, either from using JS developer tools or a previous language. It is one of the most useful tools in a developer's toolkit. While in code view (sources tab in Chrome) you can add a breakpoint by clicking the line count, which leaves a marker (the breakpoint). As I explained earlier, this default type of breakpoint pauses the JavaScript and allows you to see the current state, including the values of the variables. There are a few other types of breakpoints and not all debuggers can deal with all types of breakpoints, which can be useful in different situations.

- **DOM breakpoints:** These let you pause the code for changes such as modification of an attribute or removal of an element. In Chrome this can be found by right-clicking a DOM none and selecting one of the options listed under Break on....

- **Exceptions:** Quite often you will have code that is set up to throw an exception but rather than handling it in the code, you will want to debug it properly and figure out what caused the exception. Instead of having breakpoints on every exception, which soon gets annoying, you can set the debugger to pause on either all exceptions or just uncaught exceptions. In Chrome this is accessed by clicking the pause button that has a hexagonal background. The color changes dependent on which mode it is set to.

- **Events:** Breakpoints can be set for when an event gets triggered, such as click or mousemove, which can be very useful for making sure events are triggered where they should be and that they do as expected. In Chrome, these are available from the sources panel under the Event Listener Breakpoints heading.

- **Conditional breakpoints:** These are the same as the default breakpoint except that you can set conditions on which the breakpoint pauses, which work the same way as if you put a breakpoint within an `if` statement. These are, in my opinion, the most useful kind of breakpoint because you can use them to only pause the code when the results are not what you would expect them to be. To place a conditional breakpoint, right-click the line count and it will give you a text field to type the condition as shown in Figure 1-1.

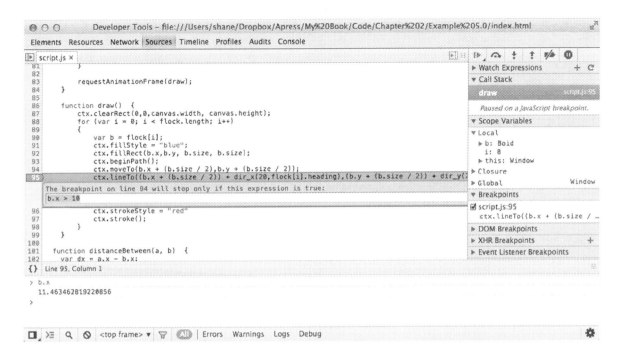

Figure 1-1. *Adding a conditional breakpoint*

Timeline

So far we have discussed functionality in debuggers that allow you to fix code and make sure it is working as you would expect it to. Sometimes however, getting the code to work is the easy bit—making it fast is often far harder. We are still on the subject of debuggers but now rather than inspecting to make sure each part of the code is working, we instead need to record the entire process so that we can spot patterns in performance (looking at the overall running of the code rather than each individual function/line). This is a subject that could easily fill an entire book, so I will go over the basics and it should give you a good starting point for figuring out how to understand and improve the performance.

In Chrome, the tool that we use to measure performance of the code is the timeline. I should note that the network pane is also related, as it lets us see which resources are causing a delay. But I'm going to focus on the running of the code rather than the resources, because it is more likely that you have experience with resources (on a normal website) than with performance testing of the code (crucial for the more creative of web apps).

To start using the timeline, you need to record the running of the code by clicking the circle button. As soon as it starts recording you will notice that some graphs are created. There are (at the time of writing) three aspects that are recorded: Events, Frames, and Memory; all these are recorded simultaneously but can only be viewed separately by selecting them. At the basic level, these features give you a good way to test the speed of parts of your code because it breaks down the code like a stack, showing you each function call. This is a fairly easy way to find bottlenecks, but it only really scratches the surface of what the timeline can do.

Rather than just showing the amount of time the function takes, it also splits it into loading, scripting, rendering, and painting. These are extremely useful for knowing why a function is taking longer than it should. The loading category is where any XHR (AJAX) calls are made as well as parsing the HTML. The logic within the function is included in the scripting category. Rendering is where the DOM manipulation takes place, primarily recalculating styles and layout. Paint is where the browser updates what is being shown to match the outcome of the rendering, including any changes on canvas and other elements that are not directly DOM related.

In Chapter 2, we use canvas for a simulation of birds flocking (known as Boids) and so I have recorded that using the timeline to show you how it works. Figure 1-2 shows the events timeline, useful for timing functions and visually seeing the stack that they produce. There are only two different colors shown in the screenshots. This is because there are very few DOM elements due to using a canvas and so there is no loading and rendering required. The lack of DOM is also the same reason for the patterns within the timeline, if we were recording performance of a regular website, then we might see changes on scrolling or hovering over a button; so the timeline is definitely powerful for more than canvas animations! Figure 1-3 shows the frames timeline. This measures the Frames Per Second (FPS) of the page because a low FPS can make a site or animation look "janky" instead of the smooth experience that people expect. The third screenshot of this section, Figure 1-4, shows the memory timeline; you can see from the spikes that the memory stores more and more until the garbage collector comes along and clears the memory that is storing old data. You will notice that there is quite a lot of whitespace below the timeline. This space is for a graph showing the amount of DOM nodes and event handlers (as you can see in Figure 1-5, which shows the timeline for a basic portfolio website I once made).

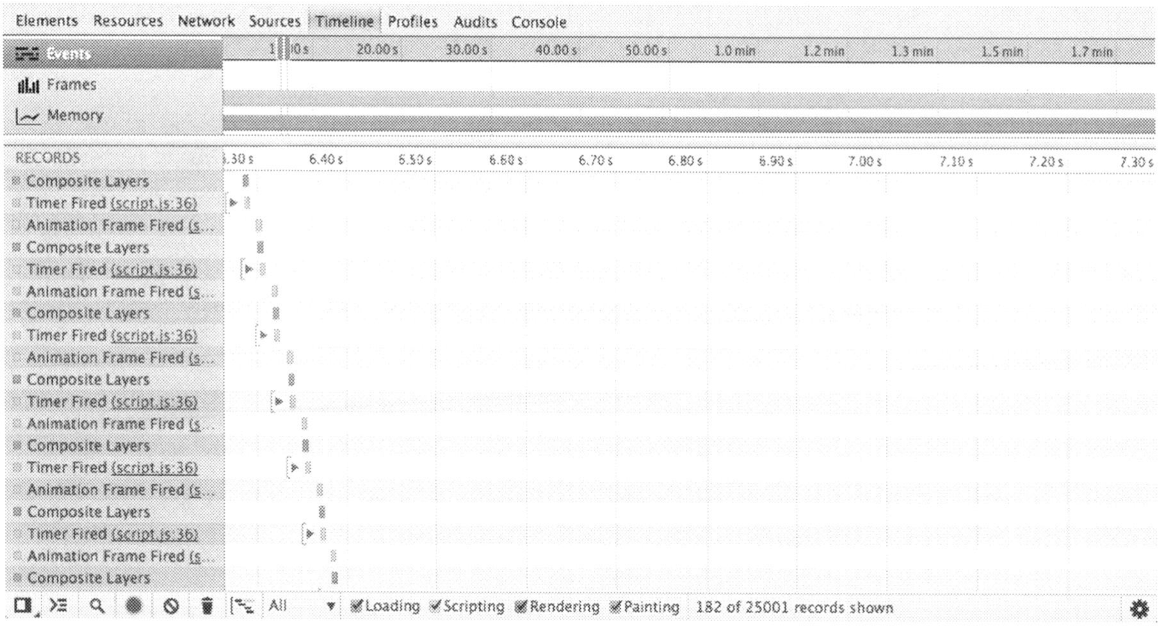

Figure 1-2. *Showing Chrome Developer Tools' events timeline*

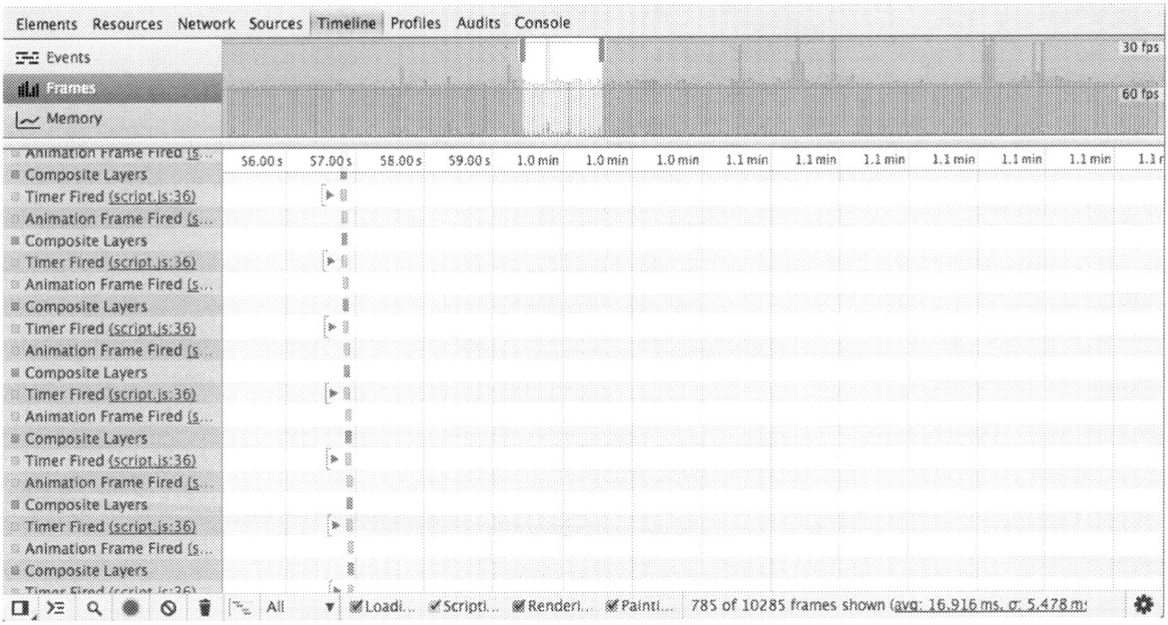

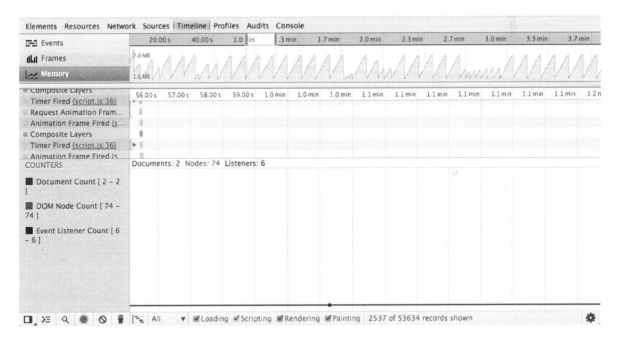

Figure 1-3. *Showing Chrome Developer Tools' frames timeline*

Figure 1-4. *Showing Chrome Developer Tools' memory timeline*

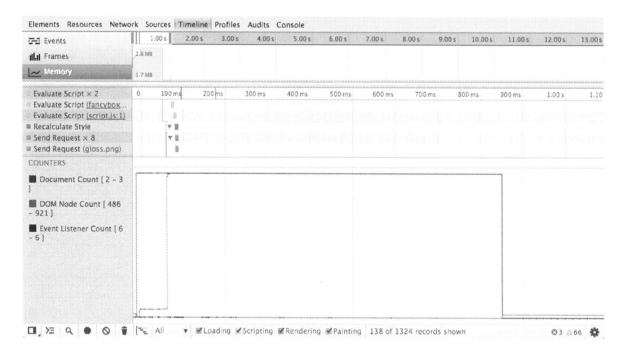

Figure 1-5. *A memory timeline showing DOM elements rendering on a portfolio website*

Canvas Profiles

The timeline is an incredibly powerful tool, but when it comes to debugging a canvas animation it can often feel like guess work (because most animations are scripted to be dynamic, we don't really know what each function is actually doing). Luckily, there is a brand new tool in Chrome Developer Tools that lets you capture a canvas frame (at the time of writing it is still only in the Canary version of Chrome). It is available under the Profiles tab (you may need to enable the experiment under the developer tools' settings).

A captured frame profile is very similar to a breakpoint, except instead of pausing the code it records a frame and allows you to step through each call that is made. This is incredibly powerful because it lets you see the exact order of execution and shows the state of the canvas at that particular step, as shown in Figure 1-6.

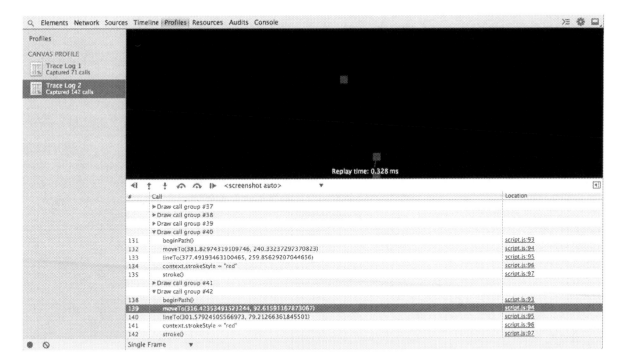

Figure 1-6. *Capturing a canvas frame*

Summary

This opening chapter has hopefully prepared you for the rest of the book. I am a strong believer that you cannot learn by purely reading a book, so I have written in such a way that I hope to guide you to different techniques and ways of learning about each subject rather than writing a "how to" book. So the debugging section of this chapter should be very useful to you throughout the rest of the book because debugging isn't just about fixing broken code, it is about exploring how the code actually works and how you can improve it.

CHAPTER 2

Canvas and Animation Basics

In the world of interactivity, a simple animation can be both a great introduction to learning as well as effective for conveying messages to the user. Many people believe that all interactive features on websites are games, but this just is not true! I hope that from this chapter you will gain an insight of how you can do something a little bit differently—how to stand out from the standard websites with professional animations.

There are many ways we can add animation these days, with the ever-more impressive HTML and CSS technologies, including: transforms, canvas, and SVG. I focus on canvas as it is used heavily throughout the book, though you should feel comfortable using all three and understand the pros and cons of each. In brief, you can think of canvas as raster and SVG as vector, with transforms used to manipulate DOM elements.

What Is Canvas?

Canvas is well named, as it can be likened to a painter's canvas because it is empty until you start painting. On its own, canvas is no different than a div—it is a blank non-semantic block element. The difference however is that canvas has a *context* that can be used for drawing on with JavaScript, this context can be extracted using var ctx = canvas. getContext('2d'); where canvas is a variable containing reference to a canvas element. You may have noticed that I have specified a 2d context, getContext allows you to choose between multiple contexts, currently the 2d context is the most common and most well developed; however WebGL and other technologies can be used for a 3d context.

Because canvas is not supported in legacy browsers, it is possible to declare a fallback so that other content can be shown instead—such as a static image or a flash animation. To add a fallback you simply just write html between the canvas tags. I would recommend you avoid writing "Canvas is not supported in your browser" because the experience of a website should be tailored to the capabilities of the device/browser rather than to criticize the user for their browsing habits; however for simplicity's sake I will be breaking that rule for many exercises in this book.

```
<canvas id="animation">
    <img src="images/canvas-fallback.png">
</canvas>
```

Once you have a context, you can start drawing. All drawing features of the context use the Cartesian grid system in which you have both the x and y axes, it should be noted that—as with most computer-based graphics—the context uses the bottom-right quadrant, so the top-left corner is its origin (0,0).

```
var ctx = canvas.getContext('2d');
//fillRect(x, y, width, height);
ctx.fillRect(10, 10, 50, 50);
```

The preceding code paints a 50px × 50px square at 10px away from the top-left corner on each axis. Do note that any four-sided shapes are called rectangles in canvas. By default this rectangle is black. Because the drawing onto context is procedural, it is required that we change color before we draw the object. After we have changed the color, all objects will use the same color until it is changed again.

```
// This sets the fill color to red
ctx.fillStyle = "#ff0000";

// fillRectangle(x, y, width, height);
ctx.fillRect(10, 10, 50, 50);
```

As you can see in Figure 2-1, the preceding code simply draws the same rectangle in red.

Figure 2-1. *A simple red rectangle*

So now, since we are concerned with animation, let's get this square moving!

RequestAnimationFrame

If you have ever needed repetitive tasks in JavaScript, such as polling, then you will probably have experience with setInterval and setTimeout. Both of these functions are unreliable because they can trigger at anytime after the timeout rather than on it, which can cause trouble if you need them to be triggered immediately (something that is quite important for smooth animations). Also, many browsers have a minimum timer resolution of about 16ms that can cause delays especially when not expected. Another problem with using timeouts is that you need to set the timeout manually; so any testing will be specific to that computer. On the other hand, requestAnimationFrame (rAF) can be used to trigger at the best time for the computer it is running on. Rather than a set time, it runs up to 60 frames per second but fires less frequently (such as when the browser tab is in the background). A further optimization that can be used is the second parameter, which can be a DOM element to constrain the rAF.

Due to a lack of browser support of requestAnimationFrame in some browsers at the time of writing, it is recommended to use a shim so that it works across browsers that implement a version of it. I will not be including this in the code examples, but you should take it as required until all browsers support the standards correctly.

```
// Shim for RequestAnimationFrame
(function() {
  var requestAnimationFrame = window.requestAnimationFrame || window.mozRequestAnimationFrame ||
                        window.webkitRequestAnimationFrame || window.msRequestAnimationFrame;
  window.requestAnimationFrame = requestAnimationFrame;
})();
```

I find that it is important to separate code, so while I will not be using any particular design patterns yet (being small amounts of code), I encourage you to organize your code appropriately. For this section I think logic() and draw() are appropriate names for functions.

```
// This is a way of selecting
var ele = document.querySelector("#animation");
var ctx = ele.getContext('2d');
var x = y = 10;
var width = height = 50;

function logic () {
    x += 10;
    if (x < ele.width - width) requestAnimationFrame(draw);
}

function draw()  {
    ctx.clearRect(0, 0, ele.width, ele.height);

    // This sets the fill colour to red
    ctx.fillStyle = "#ff0000";

    // fillRectangle(x, y, width, height);
    ctx.fillRect(x, y, 50, 50);
}

requestAnimationFrame(draw);
setInterval(logic, 1000/60);
```

You will notice that I have used both requestAnimationFrame and setInterval, this is due to the fact that you rarely want the animation to be running at full speed (dependent on the computer) so this allows the speed to be set while still using requestAnimationFrame to improve the performance of the rendering. Now, I mentioned animation does not have to run at full speed, but I have not yet showed you how to easily change that speed–for that we are going to use Linear Interpolation.

Linear Interpolation

Linear Interpolation (lerp) is used to define subcoordinates of the particular path. This can be likened to taking a long journey and stopping off for food along the way. In animation, it is used to smooth out the path, so instead of jumping from one point to another it appears to slide between them (of course, it actually just makes much smaller jumps).

```
n = start + (end - start) * speed
```

The preceding code equation is used to work out the next point of the interpolation. This should be iterated so that every frame the start variable is the n of the previous frame, because it is gradually moving toward the end point (now dependent on the speed set rather than the fps).

```
var ele = document.querySelector("#animation");
var ctx = ele.getContext('2d');
var startX = 10;
var startY = 10;
var endX = ele.width - 50;
```

```
var x = startX;
var y = startY;
var duration = 0;
var width = height = 50;

function lerp(start, end, speed) {
    return start + (end - start) * speed;
}

function logic () {
    duration += 0.02;
    x = lerp(startX, endX, duration);
    if (x < ele.width - width)
        requestAnimationFrame(draw);
}

function draw()  {
    ctx.clearRect(0, 0, ele.width, ele.height);

    // This sets the fill colour to red
    ctx.fillStyle = "#ff0000";

    // fillRectangle(x, y, width, height);
    ctx.fillRect(x, y, 50, 50);
}
requestAnimationFrame(draw);
setInterval(logic, 1000/60);
```

This is not too different from the previous version, except we now have a lerp() function almost identical to the earlier equation. I have also defined duration, startX, and startY variables to be plugged into the function. The biggest change is logic(). Rather than adjusting x (which causes it to jump), I increased duration by a tiny amount, which I then simply plugged into the lerp() function to get the new value for x (which is somewhere on the path to the final x destination).

Follow the Mouse

Quite often, you will need interactive animation rather than just a video. A common way to add interactivity within canvas is by using the mouse. To start with, I will show you how you can get your little red square to follow your movements.

The mouse is handled by the operating system and so triggers an event for all programs to access, which means of course that the term "mouse" actually means any device capable of triggering the event. For this case, we need to look for the event 'mousemove'. To do so, we use addEventListener to add the listener to a specific element.

```
element.addEventListener(type, listener, useCapture boolean optional);
```

Type is the name of the event (see the list that follows of mouse-specific events). Listener can be implemented in two ways, either as an object that implements EventListener or as a simple callback function. The useCapture is a Boolean that is true if the event should be triggered on the capture stage; otherwise it will be triggered on target and bubbling phases. useCapture will default to false on modern browsers though some older browsers will require it.

```
click
dblclick
mousedown
mouseenter
mouseleave
mousemove
mouseover
mouseout
mouseup
```

To make the mouse move, you need a callback that sets the new start and end points based on the mouse, like so:

```
ele.addEventListener('mousemove', function(evt) {
    startX = x;
    endX = evt.clientX;
});
```

This sets the new path for the square, so now we just need to modify it slightly so that it is smooth. I have decided to add constraints to make sure the square doesn't try to go off the canvas or glitch if the mouse sets x to where the square is already heading. If it doesn't match this constraint, then duration gets set to 0.

```
function logic (evt) {
    var max = ele.width - width;
    duration += 0.02;
    var l = lerp(startX, endX, duration);
    if (l < max && l > 0 && endX != x)
    {
        x = l;
        requestAnimationFrame(draw);
    }
    else {
        duration = 0;
    }
}
```

This should show you just how easily a few tiny changes can completely change the whole animation and how the user interacts with it. See Listing 2-1 to see how it all fits together.

Listing 2-1.

```
<!DOCTYPE html>
<html>
    <head>
        <title>Chapter 2 - Basics of Canvas</title>
    </head>

    <body>
        <canvas id="animation">
            <p>Fallback not supported.</p>
        </canvas>
        <script src="script.js"></script>
    </body>
</html>
```

```javascript
// Polyfill for RequestAnimationFrame
(function() {
  var requestAnimationFrame = window.requestAnimationFrame || window.mozRequestAnimationFrame ||
                              window.webkitRequestAnimationFrame || window.msRequestAnimationFrame;
  window.requestAnimationFrame = requestAnimationFrame;
})();

var ele = document.querySelector("#animation");
var ctx = ele.getContext('2d');
var width = height = 50;
var startX = 10;
var startY = 10;
var endX;
var x = startX;
var y = startY;
var duration = 0;

function logic (evt) {
    var max = ele.width - width;
    duration += 0.02;
    var l = lerp(startX, endX, duration);
    if (l < max && l > 0 && endX != x)
    {
        x = l;
        requestAnimationFrame(draw);
    }
    else {
        duration = 0;
    }
}

function draw()  {
    ctx.clearRect(0, 0, ele.width, ele.height);

    // This sets the fill colour to red
    ctx.fillStyle = "#ff0000";

    // fillRectangle(x, y, width, height);
    ctx.fillRect(x, y, 50, 50);
}

function lerp(start, end, speed) {
    return start + (end - start) * speed;
}

ele.addEventListener('mousemove', function(evt) {
    startX = x;
    endX = evt.clientX;
});

requestAnimationFrame(draw);
setInterval(logic, 1000/60);
```

Bouncing Box

Now that we have looked at how to animate in a static way (moving from left to right) as well as using an input, I would like to do one more example using the box by adding a dynamic element to it. There are so many options for how an animation works. The most common is bouncing an object off the boundaries of the canvas. It is not much of a step up in difficulty from the previous example but will tie in nicely with the next example (which will be a naïve implementation of flocking boids).

Instead of "lerping" between current and desired positions, to bounce a box we need to make it go in a specific direction until it hits an edge. This means that we need to use basic trigonometry to take an angle (it will begin as a random angle under 360 degrees) and to find the position. As you know from lerping, it is best to move in lots of small steps rather than a big one, so we can define the distance for the trigonometry function to find. To find the x direction, we find the cos of the angle (in radians) multiplied by the distance and for the y direction we do the same but using the sin of the angle.

```
function degreesToRadians(degrees) {
    return degrees * (Math.PI / 180);
}

function dir_x(length, angle) {
    return length * Math.cos(degreesToRadians(angle));
}

function dir_y(length, angle) {
    return length * Math.sin(degreesToRadians(angle));
}
```

Once we implement these functions, it is similar to the previous examples. We need to initialize variables for both x and y axes for distance and heading (direction). Distance should start as 0, and heading needs to be a random angle up to 360 degrees. Within logic, it is best to start with a simple check to make sure both heading variables are between −360 and 360. Then we need to check whether the object is within the boundaries, if it isn't, then bounce it back. After that, we simply lerp between current position and the position that is found by using the degrees and direction functions above.

```
var ele = document.querySelector("#animation");
ele.height = window.innerHeight;
ele.width = window.innerWidth;
var ctx = ele.getContext('2d');
var x = 10;
var y = 10;
var duration = 0;
var width = height = 50;
var heading_x = heading_y = Math.random() * 360;
var distance_x = distance_y = 0;

function logic () {
    if (heading_x > 360 || heading_x < -360) heading_x = 0;
    if (heading_y > 360 || heading_y < -360) heading_y = 0;

    if (x <= 0 || x >=ele.width - width) {
        heading_x = heading_x + 180;
    }
```

```
    if (y <= 0 || y >=ele.height - height) {
        heading_y = -heading_y;
    }

    distance_x = dir_x(2, heading_x);
    distance_y = dir_y(2, heading_y);
    if (duration < 10) duration += 0.05;
    x = lerp(x, x + distance_x, duration);
    y = lerp(y, y + distance_y, duration);
    requestAnimationFrame(draw);
}
```

And that's that. You can find the full code listing for all the examples in the download that complements this book on the Apress website at www.apress.com/9781430259442 or my own website at www.shanehudson.net/javascript-creativity.

"Clever" Animation

Next we are going to create a "clever" animation–that is to say, extending on the previous concept of dynamic animation found in the bouncing box example by making objects aware of their surroundings. In 1986, Craig Reynolds created an incredible simulation of birds flocking that he called Boids. It was built on just three rules that allowed each boid to be responsible for its own movement, but also allowed it to see local neighbors and move toward them. The best explanation for each rule I have found was this:

- **Separation**: Steer to avoid crowding local flockmates
- **Alignment**: Steer toward the average heading of local flockmates
- **Cohesion**: Steer to move toward the average position (center of mass) of local flockmates

Our animation is based on Boids, though some of it will be simplified for brevity (I encourage you to modify my code to improve it–to do so you will probably want to use vectors). We will start with our usual set up code, getContext. etc., as well as creating an object for Boid that holds the data about location, direction, and size of the boid. Once that is done we create a function called setup(), which adds each boid (depending how many we set) onto the canvas at a random position with a random direction. I have made a simple function to wrap the JavaScript Math.random, just to make the code a bit neater.

```
(function() {
  var canvas = document.querySelector("#flocking");
  var ctx = canvas.getContext('2d');

  canvas.height = window.innerHeight;
  canvas.width = window.innerWidth;
  var flock = [];

  var flockRadius = 250;
  var neighborRadius = 10;

  var Boid = function(x, y, heading, size) {

    this.x = x;
    this.y = y;
```

```
    this.heading = heading
    this.size = size;

};

function setup() {
  for (var i = 0; i < 50; i++)
  {
      flock.push(new Boid(rand(canvas.width), rand(canvas.height), rand(360), 15));
  }
  setInterval(logic, 1000/60);
}

function logic () {
  for (var i = 0; i < flock.length; i++) {
    // Do something with each boid
  }
  requestAnimationFrame(draw);
}

function draw() {
  // Drawing goes here
}

function rand(max) {
  return Math.random() * max;
}
setup();
})();
```

You may notice that for direction instead of "up" or "right" we use degrees, 0 to 360. This makes the animation much more fluid and also allows us to use radian math later. We use a variable flockRadius to control the distance at which boids can see each other (used for heading the same way, etc.). Now let's add some code to the drawing method. For this we are going to need to start by clearing the canvas each frame (if you don't do this, you will just draw over the previous frame). Once the canvas is cleared, it is time to draw the boids! So we need to iterate over the flock array, while storing the current boid in a variable called b, drawing each one to the canvas (that is, the context of the canvas) at the correct position. To find the position, we take b.x and b.y but we need to add half of its size onto it, because the position is the center of the boid rather than the top left of it.

```
function draw() {
  ctx.clearRect(0,0,canvas.width, canvas.height);
  for (var i = 0; i < flock.length; i++)
  {
    var b = flock[i];
      ctx.fillStyle = "blue";
      ctx.fillRect(b.x,b.y, b.size, b.size);
      ctx.beginPath();
      ctx.moveTo(b.x + (b.size / 2),b.y + (b.size / 2));
```

```
        ctx.lineTo((b.x + (b.size / 2)) + dir_x(20,flock[i].heading),(b.y + (b.size / 2)) +
dir_y(20,flock[i].heading));
        ctx.strokeStyle = "red"
        ctx.stroke();
    }
}
```

In lineTo I have used a couple of functions used to get the position when given a distance and direction. In this case I have used the functions to draw a line pointing 20px in the direction each boid is heading. Here you can see the helper functions. They use basic trigonometry and Pythagoras, so they should be fairly easy to follow.

```
function distanceBetween(a, b)  {
  var dx = a.x - b.x;
  var dy = a.y - b.y;
  return Math.sqrt(dx * dx + dy * dy);
}

function angleBetween(x1, y1, x2, y2)
{
  return Math.atan2(y1 - y2, x1 - x2) * (180.0 / Math.PI);
}

function angleDifference(a1, a2)
{
  return ((((a1 - a2) % 360) + 540) % 360) - 180;
}

function degreesToRadians(degrees){
    return degrees * (Math.PI / 180);
}

function dir_x(length, angle){
  return length * Math.cos(degreesToRadians(angle));
}

function dir_y(length, angle){
  return length * Math.sin(degreesToRadians(angle));
}
```

Don't be put off by all the math–it just makes it much easier to write our logic function, which we are going to do now! We need to start by setting up some variables within the for loop for the position of where the boid is headed. This is called centerx and centery, but it is not the center of the canvas (I think of it as the "center of attention"). I also provide a variable b to make it easier to access flock[i]. With the variables set up, we can now loop through the boids again to find the neighbors, which is any boid within a distance of less than flockRadius. With these we can find the average position (adding the x and y of each boid to centerx and centery, then dividing by the amount of boids in the radius). Of course, if there is only one boid in the flock we might as well give it a random position to head toward.

```
for (var i = 0; i < flock.length; i++)  {
  var centerx = 0;
  var centery = 0;
  var count = 0;
```

```
  var b = flock[i];

  for (var j = 0; j < flock.length; j++)
  {
    var distance = distanceBetween(b, flock[j]);
      if (distance < flockRadius)
      {
        centerx += flock[j].x;
        centery += flock[j].y;
        count++;
      }
  }

  if (count > 1) {
    centerx = centerx / count;
    centery = centery / count;
  }
  else {
    centerx = Math.random() * canvas.width;
    centery = Math.random() * canvas.height;
  }
  // Set heading and x/y positions
}
```

Now that we have our center of attention/gravity (I suppose gravity is a better word for it) we can work out the angle the boid needs to turn to head in the correct direction. We do this by using the angleBetween and angleDifference helper functions to get the angle needed, then linear interpolating it so that every iteration it gets closer to the point it is heading. Of course, due to the way we have set up the code, the point it is heading to may change depending on its proximity to its neighbors (remember we change the center point in the nested loop). Lastly, so that the boids don't just fly off the page, we need to define a "wrap around" so that if the boid goes off the canvas it appears on the opposite side (just like Asteroids or Snake).

```
if (count > 1) {
  centerx = centerx / count;
  centery = centery / count;
}
else {
  centerx = Math.random() * canvas.width;
  centery = Math.random() * canvas.height;
}

var angleToCenter = angleBetween(b.x,b.y,centerx,centery);
var lerpangle = angleDifference(b.heading, angleToCenter);

b.heading += lerpangle * 0.01;

headingx = dir_x(2,b.heading);
headingy = dir_y(2,b.heading);

b.x += headingx;
b.y += headingy;
```

```
if (b.x < 0) b.x = canvas.width;
if (b.y < 0) b.y = canvas.height;

if (b.x > canvas.width) b.x = 0;
if (b.y > canvas.height) b.y = 0;
```

If you put the above code where the comment was on the previous code, you should find that you now have blue boids with red lines, indicating direction, which fly around the canvas and join groups. Figure 2-2 shows how this should look. The animation can be improved in a number of ways, such as adding separation so they fly next to each other rather than through one another.

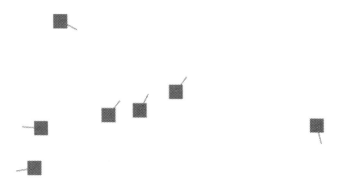

Figure 2-2. *This shows each boid heading a specific direction. Also note the three boids in the middle heading the same way as a flock*

In listing 2-2 you can see the full code for this example, which is available for download online as with the previous examples.

Listing 2-2.

```
(function()  {
  var canvas = document.querySelector("#flocking");
  var ctx = canvas.getContext('2d');

  canvas.height = window.innerHeight;
  canvas.width = window.innerWidth;
  var flock = [];

  var flockRadius = 250;

  var Boid = function(x, y, heading, size) {

    this.x = x;
    this.y = y;
    this.heading = heading
    this.size = size;

  };
```

```
    function setup()  {
      for (var i = 0; i < 50; i++)
      {
        flock.push(new Boid(Math.random() * canvas.width, Math.random() * canvas.height, Math.random()
* 360, 15));
      }
      setInterval(logic, 1000/60);
    }

    function logic () {

      for (var i = 0; i < flock.length; i++)  {
        var centerx = 0;
        var centery = 0;
        var count = 0;

        var b = flock[i];

        for (var j = 0; j < flock.length; j++)
        {
          var distance = distanceBetween(b, flock[j]);
          if (distance < flockRadius)
          {
            centerx += flock[j].x;
            centery += flock[j].y;
            count++;
          }
        }

        if (count > 1) {
          centerx = centerx / count;
          centery = centery / count;
        }
        else  {
          centerx = Math.random() * canvas.width;
          centery = Math.random() * canvas.height;
        }

        var angleToCenter = angleBetween(b.x,b.y,centerx,centery);
        var lerpangle = angleDifference(b.heading, angleToCenter);

        b.heading += lerpangle * 0.01;

        headingx = dir_x(2,b.heading);
        headingy = dir_y(2,b.heading);

        b.x += headingx;
        b.y += headingy;

        if (b.x < 0) b.x = canvas.width;
        if (b.y < 0) b.y = canvas.height;
```

```
      if (b.x > canvas.width) b.x = 0;
      if (b.y > canvas.height) b.y = 0;
    }

    requestAnimationFrame(draw);
  }

  function draw()  {
    ctx.clearRect(0,0,canvas.width, canvas.height);
    for (var i = 0; i < flock.length; i++)
    {
      var b = flock[i];
      ctx.fillStyle = "blue";
      ctx.fillRect(b.x,b.y, b.size, b.size);
      ctx.beginPath();
      ctx.moveTo(b.x + (b.size / 2),b.y + (b.size / 2));
      ctx.lineTo((b.x + (b.size / 2)) + dir_x(20,flock[i].heading),(b.y + (b.size / 2)) +
dir_y(20,flock[i].heading));
      ctx.strokeStyle = "red"
      ctx.stroke();
    }
  }

  function distanceBetween(a, b)  {
    var dx = a.x - b.x;
    var dy = a.y - b.y;
    return Math.sqrt(dx * dx + dy * dy);
  }

  function angleBetween(x1, y1, x2, y2)
  {
    return Math.atan2(y1 - y2, x1 - x2) * (180.0 / Math.PI);
  }

  function angleDifference(a1, a2)
  {
    return ((((a1 - a2) % 360) + 540) % 360) - 180;
  }

  function degreesToRadians(degrees){
    return degrees * (Math.PI / 180);
  }

  function dir_x(length, angle){
    return length * Math.cos(degreesToRadians(angle));
  }

  function dir_y(length, angle){
    return length * Math.sin(degreesToRadians(angle));
  }

  setup();

})();
```

Introducing Drag-and-Drop

Quite often you will want to use drag-and-drop as part of an animation or as an integral part of your application. This might be for dragging elements around the page to trigger an event, or it might be to drag files from your system into the browser. I am going to introduce using a rather advanced app that works similar to a coloring book where you drag an image onto the canvas and it generates line art that the user can color in. Both of these are good examples of how we can create impressive interfaces using modern HTML, as well as prove that these technologies are not just for game creation!

As mentioned, I am going to demonstrate the technique of dragging local files into the browser by creating a small coloring book web app where dragging an image onto the canvas turns it into line art that can then be colored in using a brush. My reason for making an app like this is to both get you thinking about slightly more advanced techniques, such as edge detection, but more importantly I want you to have something you can fiddle with, and extend functionality to your heart's desire—the only way to learn is to do. So throughout both this mini-project and, indeed, the entire book, I will be providing ideas and mentioning algorithms for you to think about and implement.

For our coloring book we need to start with a full-size canvas. This is done through JavaScript, because setting 100% width and height via CSS would scale rather than increase the size of the canvas. We also need to set up event listeners for 'dragover', 'dragenter', and 'drop' events. For the first two events we need to stop the default browser behavior, so I have created a simple function called preventDefault, .which calls a method with the same name on the event. In Listing 2-3, you can see the boilerplate code for setting up the canvas to enable drag and drop functionality.

Listing 2-3.

```
<!DOCTYPE html>
<html>
    <head>
        <title>Coloring Book</title>
    </head>

    <body style="margin:0">
        <canvas id="drop"></canvas>
    </body>
    <script>

(function() {
    var drop = document.querySelector("#drop");
    var ctx = drop.getContext('2d');

    /* These are to set the canvas to full width */
    drop.height = window.innerHeight;
    drop.width = window.innerWidth;

    drop.addEventListener('dragover', preventDefault);
    drop.addEventListener('dragenter', preventDefault);
    drop.addEventListener('drop', handleDrop);

    function preventDefault(e) {
      if (e.preventDefault) {
        e.preventDefault();
      }
      return false;
    }
```

```
    function handleDrop(e) {
      e.stopPropagation();
      e.preventDefault();
      e.dataTransfer.dropEffect = "copy";
      // Code for drop will go here
    }

})();
</script>
</html>
```

As you can see in Listing 2-3, this provides a good starting point, but now we need to actually put the image onto the canvas. All the data that we need to use is stored in e, the event variable of handleDrop, so we can move the file itself into its own variable–which I have aptly named 'file'–using e.dataTransfer.files[0]; which gives us the first of the dropped files (as in this example we will only be using one). Of course, you could extend this by making each dropped file open in a separate canvas such as Photoshop does.

Due to the way it is implemented, to draw an image to the canvas you must first put it into an HTML element; this is slightly odd but easy to work with once you know about it as luckily the element does not need to be added to the DOM. We also require a FileReader to do two things: first to turn the file into a base 64 data URL and second to add the data URL to the src of the image element once the file has loaded.

```
var file = e.dataTransfer.files[0];
var image = new Image();

var reader = new FileReader();
reader.readAsDataURL(file);

reader.onload = (function() {
  return function(e)  {
    image.src = e.target.result;
  };
})();
```

So now the image exists and is sitting in image.src, but we cannot yet see it because it hasn't been added to the DOM or drawn to the canvas. Time to fix that! In the same way that reader had an onload event handler attribute, so does image. So we just need to write a function that draws the image to the **context of the canvas** at the top-left corner of the canvas (aka (0,0)). This is done like this:

```
function handleDrop(e) {
  e.stopPropagation();
  e.preventDefault();
  e.dataTransfer.dropEffect = "copy";

  var file = e.dataTransfer.files[0];
  var image = new Image();

  var reader = new FileReader();
  reader.readAsDataURL(file);
```

```
  reader.onload = (function() {
    return function(e)  {
       image.src = e.target.result;
    };
  })();

  image.onload = function() {
   ctx.drawImage(image, 0, 0);
   };
}
```

Now if you copy that into the module, you should be able to drop images onto the page and have them appear on the canvas!

We are now going to write a "naïve" edge detection filter loosely based on the Sobel operator, this implementation of the filter is based on an example within the html spec for pixel manipulation (our version reduces the colors to black and white lines). There is a more advanced version that uses Sobel called Canny Edge Detection (developed in 1986 by John F. Canny). This is one feature that you might want to add yourself because it includes noise reduction and so can produce much higher quality line art.

Let's start by creating a new function called findEdges that takes a parameter called originalData, which should hold the image data of the context; that is, a copy of the current context state that is being shown on the canvas (in this case, our image). Within the function we should create a variable, let's call it output, to hold the temporary image data that we will be writing each pixel to so that it can then be put back onto the context. Now, another odd thing you need to remember, to write pixels to the image data you have to have two variables, one for the 'ImageData' (our output variable) and one for the 'ImageData.data' (let's call this outputData), which sounds silly, but both are tightly coupled so you write to outputData then put the output (automatically containing the correct data) onto the canvas context. Before we get into the edge detection algorithm I am going to show you the code for all this set-up code.

```
function findEdges(originalData) {
    var output = ctx.createImageData(drop.width, drop.height);

    var w = originalData.width, h = originalData.height;
    var inputData = originalData.data;
    var outputData = output.data;
    var threshold = 100;

    // edge detection goes here

    // put the image data back after manipulation
    ctx.putImageData(output, 0, 0);
}
```

To write the algorithm you first need to understand the data structure, which is a Uint8ClampedArray. Although the name sounds quite scary, it is an array of 8-bit unsigned (positive only) integers (or as I prefer–byte-sized elements!) that is quite simply organized as a pattern of 'red, green, blue, alpha' which then repeats itself, so that each pixel is made up of four array elements.

To work out the position (i) of the pixel, we need two loops, one for the height (y) of the image and another for the width (x). We can then get the first color (red) of each pixel by working out y times width of the canvas, since the array stores by row, then add x to find the position in that row. Of course, this is then multiplied by 4 due to the amount of colors (including alpha) that make up the pixel.

```
for (var y = 0; y < h; y += 1) {
  for (var x = 0; x < w; x += 1) {
    var i = (y * w + x) * 4;
  }
}
```

Now that we have worked out the position of each pixel we need to work out the weighted average, which we can do by adding all the neighboring (both directional and diagonal) colors then subtracting 8 times the current color since there are 8 neighbors. Once that is done, we set all colors in the pixel (including alpha) to 255 or 0 depending on which side of the threshold they are. The threshold I set earlier to 100 but you are welcome to fiddle around with the numbers to find the best result. After this we just put the output (the ImageData) onto the context of the canvas.

```
image.onload = function() {
    ctx.drawImage(image, 0, 0);
    var originalData = ctx.getImageData(0, 0, drop.width, drop.height);
    findEdges(originalData);
  };
function findEdges(originalData) {
  var output = ctx.createImageData(drop.width, drop.height);

  var w = originalData.width, h = originalData.height;
  var inputData = originalData.data;
  var outputData = output.data;
  var threshold = 100;

  // edge detection
  for (var y = 0; y < h; y += 1) {
    for (var x = 0; x < w; x += 1) {
      var i = (y * w + x) * 4;
      outputData[i] = inputData[i - w*4 - 4]  +   inputData[i - w*4]  + inputData[i - w*4 + 4] +
                      inputData[i - 4]           - 8 * inputData[i]           + inputData[i + 4] +
         inputData[i + w*4 - 4] + inputData[i + w*4] + inputData[i + w*4 + 4];
      if (outputData[i] < threshold)
      {
         outputData[i] = 255;
         outputData[i+1] = 255;
         outputData[i+2] = 255;
      }
      else
      {
         outputData[i] = 0;
         outputData[i+1] = 0;
         outputData[i+2] = 0;
      }
    outputData[i + 3] = 255; // alpha
    }
 }
 // put the image data back after manipulation
 ctx.putImageData(output, 0, 0);
}
```

Now when you drag an image onto the canvas you should get a rough outline. One of your challenges, if you are willing to take it, is to improve the quality of the outline. As I mentioned earlier, your best bet is probably by implementing Canny but there are also some easier changes that can be made to improve it. Please do tweet or email me any attempts at improving the algorithm!

Making the Paintbrush

Our next task is to make a paintbrush—a round circular brush, not a modern Photoshop-style brush that includes all the bristles.

As with before, we need to decide which events need to be triggered. I think we should use mousedown to trigger drawing, mouseup to stop drawing, and mousemove to draw while the mouse is down, We can check this using a Boolean called 'drawing'. In mousedown we need to call a function, I have called it startPath, to begin the path; this needs to be done separately to the rest of the path so that it does not keep trying to start a new path every time the mouse moves. In startPath we need to begin the path, using ctx.beginPath(), then move the brush to the current position of the mouse. In canvas, and indeed most other computer graphics libraries, moveTo is used to move the brush without drawing and lineTo is used to draw from the current position to the new position. I have also used startPath to set the size and the color of the brush.

```
drop.addEventListener('mousedown', startPath);
drop.addEventListener('mouseup', function() {
  drawing = false;
});
drop.addEventListener('mousemove', handleDrawing);

function startPath(e)  {
  ctx.strokeStyle = "#0000ff";
  ctx.lineWidth    = lineWidth;
  ctx.beginPath();
  ctx.moveTo(e.clientX + lineWidth, e.clientY + lineWidth);
  drawing = true;
}
```

As you can see from the code, mousemove triggers a function called handleDrawing. This uses lineTo that I mentioned earlier to draw the path, as well calls stroke to make it the size and color specified in startPath.

```
function handleDrawing(e)  {
  if (drawing == true)
  {
    ctx.lineTo(e.clientX + lineWidth, e.clientY + lineWidth);
    ctx.stroke();
  }
}
```

Our last task is to make this image downloadable. To do this we go back to using toDataURL in the href of a link. To make the link downloadable we can use the download attribute, a new feature that is available in some modern browsers. On other browsers, the user would have to right-click and manually save the image. You can add that to the alt text to make it easy to use if you want to.

```
var save = document.querySelector("#save");
save.addEventListener('click', saveCanvas);
```

```
function saveCanvas() {
  var img = drop.toDataURL("image/png");
  save.href = img;
  save.download = "colouringBook.png";
}
```

```
<a id="save" class="button">Save</a>
```

You can see this example in its entirety below in Listing 2-4.

Listing 2-4.

```
<!DOCTYPE html>
<html>
  <head>
    <title>Coloring Book</title>
    <style>
      body {
        margin: 0;
        padding: 0;
      }
      #drop {
        display: block;
        position: absolute;
        right: 0;
        top: 0;
        z-index: 0;
      }
      .button {
        background-color: rgba(0,0,0,0.6);
        color: #fff;
        display: inline-block;
        font-family: sans-serif;
        font-size: 24px;
        font-weight: bold;
        margin: 10px 0 0 10px;
        padding: 5px;
        position: relative;
        text-transform: uppercase;
        z-index: 1;
      }
    </style>
  </head>

  <body>
    <a id="save" class="button">Save</a>
    <canvas id="drop"></canvas>
    <script src="script.js"></script>
  </body>
</html>
```

```
var colouringBook = (function() {
  var drop = document.querySelector("#drop");
  var save = document.querySelector("#save");
  var ctx = drop.getContext('2d');
  var drawing;
  var lineWidth = 5;

  /* These are to set the canvas to full width */
  drop.height = window.innerHeight;
  drop.width = window.innerWidth;

  drop.addEventListener('dragover', preventDefault);
  drop.addEventListener('dragenter', preventDefault);
  drop.addEventListener('drop', handleDrop);

  drop.addEventListener('mousedown', startPath);
  drop.addEventListener('mouseup', function() {
    drawing = false;
  });
  drop.addEventListener('mousemove', handleDrawing);

  save.addEventListener('click', saveCanvas);

  function preventDefault(e) {
    if (e.preventDefault) {
      e.preventDefault();
    }
    return false;
  }

  function handleDrop(e) {
    e.stopPropagation();
    e.preventDefault();
    e.dataTransfer.dropEffect = "copy";

    var file = e.dataTransfer.files[0];
    var image = new Image();

    var reader = new FileReader();
    reader.readAsDataURL(file);

    reader.onload = (function() {
      return function(e)  {
        image.src = e.target.result;
      };
    })();

    image.onload = function() {
      ctx.drawImage(image, 0, 0);
      var originalData = ctx.getImageData(0, 0, drop.width, drop.height);
      findEdges(originalData);
    };
  }
```

```
function findEdges(originalData) {
  var output = ctx.createImageData(drop.width, drop.height);

  var w = originalData.width, h = originalData.height;
  var inputData = originalData.data;
  var outputData = output.data;
  var threshold = 100;

  // edge detection
  for (var y = 0; y < h; y += 1) {
    for (var x = 0; x < w; x += 1) {
      var i = (y * w + x) * 4;

      outputData[i] = inputData[i - w*4 - 4] +   inputData[i - w*4] + inputData[i - w*4 + 4] +
            inputData[i - 4]        -   8*inputData[i]      + inputData[i + 4] +
            inputData[i + w*4 - 4] +   inputData[i + w*4] + inputData[i + w*4 + 4];

      if (outputData[i] < threshold)
      {
        outputData[i] = 255;
        outputData[i+1] = 255;
        outputData[i+2] = 255;
      }
      else
      {
        outputData[i] = 0;
        outputData[i+1] = 0;
        outputData[i+2] = 0;
      }
      outputData[i + 3] = 255; // alpha
    }
  }

  // put the image data back after manipulation
  ctx.putImageData(output, 0, 0);
}

function startPath(e)  {
  ctx.strokeStyle = "#0000ff";
  ctx.lineWidth   = lineWidth;
  ctx.beginPath();
  ctx.moveTo(e.clientX + lineWidth, e.clientY + lineWidth);
  drawing = true;
}

function handleDrawing(e)  {
  if (drawing == true)
  {
    ctx.lineTo(e.clientX + lineWidth, e.clientY + lineWidth);
    ctx.stroke();
  }
}
```

```
function saveCanvas() {
  var img = drop.toDataURL("image/png");
  save.href = img;
  save.download = "colouringBook.png";
}

})();
```

> ■ **Note**   You can find the full source code for this project in the download that complements the book on the Apress website at www.apress.com/9781430259442 or my own website at www.shanehudson.net/javascript-creativity/.

You now have your coloring book as shown in Figure 2-3.

Figure 2-3. *This figure shows a photo of penguins that has been turned into line art and painted on using canvas*

Summary

You should now feel confident about some of the math behind animation, such as linear interpolation. You should also feel that you understand requestAnimationFrame and generally how to set up the framework of an animation. I included some drag-and-drop because I find pure "let's paint some lines" kind of drawing examples boring. I hope this has mixed it up a bit and been useful. Both the coloring book example and boids have a massive scope of improvements (and indeed optimizations), which I encourage you to explore.

As we end this chapter, I would like to get you thinking about animation and things you can do with canvas and animation in general. We live in a world full of data. Noise. Be it statistics or tweets, it is hard to see what is important and what isn't. The web does not need to be linear. Take, for example, a Twitter timeline. . . now imagine those tweets in the form of boids, where they group each other based on perhaps author or topic, or maybe how much the hashtag is trending. Animations are not needed for everything, but they can be both decoration as well as extremely useful. I would love to see what you come up with!

CHAPTER 3

■ ■ ■

Audio and Video Basics

If we are talking about interactivity, we are going to want to use audio and video. For years we had to use "hacks" such as Flash or Silverlight to add these crucial elements to the web, but we now have audio and video built directly into HTML. In this chapter we go through the ins and outs of both elements (that is, <audio> and <video>) so that you can use them without hesitation. I also introduce you to some new techniques such as manipulation, and we will touch on optimization techniques too. In later chapters we will be exploring the depths of audio creation and we will be creating a media player in the process. This chapter gives you the grounding you need to do that.

Containers and Codecs

When it comes to using audio and video, we will be dealing with a variety of browser implementations and support. Each format tends to have a set of advantages and disadvantages, some are well optimized and some are freely licensed. For this reason, it's good to understand a little about a few containers and codecs, their limitations, and whether they are licensed, before we go on to the details of how to implement.

Containers

A container is a file format that is used as a wrapper format for a range of codecs. You could think of containers as files that hold audio that has already been encoded with a codec, as well as data on which codec was used. Many codecs are supported by multiple containers.

WebM

WebM is an audio-video container sponsored by Google. It is royalty free, and comprises VP8 video and Vorbis audio streams in a container based on Matroska. It's released under a BSD license and all users are granted a worldwide, non-exclusive, no-charge, royalty-free patent license.

MP4

The Moving Picture Experts Group (MPEG) has standardized many containers and codecs. They are probably most well-known for the MP3 audio codec, but MP4 is one of the most commonly used video formats. MP4 usually uses H.264 as the video codec and AAC or MP3 as the audio codec. The MP4 format is patent-encumbered, which has caused discussions between browsers about the suitability of non-royalty-free formats on the web.

QuickTime File Format

Safari uses QuickTime for playing formats that are not natively supported in the browser, such as QuickTime File Format (known as Mov). MP4 was based on the Mov specification and so supports the same codecs as MP4 but has less support, as MP4 is standardized and Mov is not.

AVI

Microsoft released Audio Video Interleaved (AVI) in 1992; it is one of the oldest container formats that is still widely used (alongside Mov). Because AVI is so old, it has a lot of disadvantages to the more modern containers such as MP4 and Ogg. Some disadvantages include a lack of meta-data and compression. Due to these disadvantages, AVI is not used natively on the web but can be used with Flash video players.

ASF

Advanced Systems Format (ASF) is a container that was created by Microsoft especially for streaming media. ASF usually contains either Windows Media Video (WMV) or Windows Media Audio (WMA). The specification is freely (as in beer) available but is patented-encumbered.

Ogg

Ogg is an open source container format maintained by the Xiph.Org Foundation and released under the BSD license. The format is praised highly due to how open it is, but at the time of writing Internet Explorer, Safari, and many mobile browsers do not support it. That said, it is generally recommended to use Ogg alongside other formats. Ogg supports many codecs but is usually used with Vorbis for audio and Theora for video.

Matroska

Another fully open container format is Matroska. It is a universal format in that it attempts to support all codecs (where possible). WebM is a subset of Matroska. This is so media players (including browsers) can say they support WebM without having full support for every codec that Matroska supports.

WAV

Waveform Audio File Format (known by its file extension WAV) is a container developed by Microsoft and IBM. It is patent-free and is lossless. Commonly, WAV is used as an uncompressed format but it can be used with Lossless Pulse-code modulation (LPCM) for compression.

Codecs

A codec is used to encode data, to take a raw data stream (a signal) and process it. Most codecs attempt to compress the raw data, some are lossy (meaning that the compression loses quality) and others are lossless. It is the encoded data (created by the codec) that is held within the container format.

MP3

This is probably the most well-known audio format, so it is probably a good codec to start with. MP3 is known as a lossy format, as opposed to a lossless format, meaning the sound loses quality when compressed from original the recording. However, it is well optimized and can be a good choice for audio on the web due to low bandwidth usage. The biggest downfall to MP3 is that it is patented, meaning that many people (notably Mozilla in the past, who refused to support the format until Firefox 21) are against the format and instead opt to use freely available formats.

Vorbis

Vorbis is the most popular open source, patent-free, audio codec that is supported on many browsers. It is often referred to as Ogg Vorbis despite Ogg being a container that Vorbis is often used with rather than the format's name. There are many other containers for Vorbis, but usually the container is Ogg, QuickTime MOV, or WebM.

AAC

Advanced Audio Coding (AAC) is particularly interesting as it often complements H.264 to provide audio, and is the primary audio codec used in 3GP (commonly used on mobile devices) containers (other than AMR). AAC is supported in most browsers (except Opera Firefox on OSX, and some Linux distributions due to licensing agreements).

AC-3

AC-3 is an audio codec created by Dolby Laboratories and generally known as Dolby Digital. It is rarely used on the web but is widely used in high-definition movies.

H.264

H.264 is a video codec developed by the Video Coding Experts Group (VCEG) and the Moving Picture Experts Group. The codec is used for Blu-ray discs and is also very popular on the web because browser support is good (all browsers except Opera support H.264 where possible, due to licensing issues). Cisco has released an open implementation of H.264 that attempts to solve the licensing issues.

VP8

This is the codec used for video in WebM. It is owned by Google but they have given an irrevocable patent promise that allows anyone to implement VP8.

Theora

Based on VP3 (a predecessor to VP8), Theora is an open, lossy video codec that is maintained by the Xiph.Org Foundation. It is often used on the web with the Ogg container format.

Encoding Videos

Now, you may want to know how to encode videos. Unfortunately browsers cannot automatically do this, so you will need to use a converter. There are many converters available, but the most popular seem to be Handbrake and Miro. I personally use Miro because it is well-designed, simple to use, and open source, Miro is available at `www.mirovideoconverter.com`.

Browser Compatibility

At the time of writing, Firefox has not yet added support for MP3 and both Internet Explorer and Safari do not support OGG or WebM. Mobile support is even more lacking.

As with `<audio>` there are quite a few codecs and containers we can use. Chrome and Firefox have both committed to WebM, although Internet Explorer and Safari do not support it. Some older versions of browsers will support `<audio>` but not WebM, so it is worth using OGG and MP4 too. Earlier I mentioned that Vorbis is often called OGG Vorbis, for video we use the OGG container with Vorbis for audio and Theora for video. OGG and WebM are both preferred over MP4 for the patent reasons described earlier. To see the current state of browser support, please check `www.docs.webplatform.org/wiki/html/elements/audio`.

Using the <audio> and <video> elements

Now that we have an understanding of containers and codecs and the files we may encounter, we can look at how we implement these on our web pages.

░ **Note** The audio used in this chapter is from `www.incompetech.com/music/royalty-free` and the video is from `www.bigbuckbunny.com`.

<audio>

Let's start with the audio element, which is what we use to listen to sound in modern browsers. This sound could be anything, from a podcast to music. Before we start I need to stress a point—use this with care. Don't blast out sound when the user loads the website. We hated this when Flash could do it and we still hate it now. In its most basic form, the audio element can take a `src` just like an `img` element can:

```
<audio src="audio.mp3" >
```

This is simply added into your HTML document. The problem with this is that we cannot provide a list of files, because we need to provide different audio codecs based on browser compatibility. To solve this, we use the `<source>` element nested inside `<audio>`. This is an element that allows you to provide different files and have the browser automatically choose the best case. It takes the `src` attribute like normal, as well as type. In the `type` attribute we give the MIME type (as you may expect), this needs to include both the container as the main type with the codecs included after a semicolon. You can also include a Flash alternative alongside the source elements if you deem it necessary to target older browsers. Here is an example, the audio files can be found on the Incompetech website at the link above, as well as in the download for this book:

```
<audio>
    <source src='audio.ogg' type='audio/ogg; codecs=vorbis'>
    <source src='audio.mp3' type='audio/mpeg'>
</audio>
```

Because the browsers have an algorithm to choose the source, the order of sources and the amount of them are not a problem. Most people currently just use Vorbis and MP3 but over time that may change. It is quite likely that WebM container format will become more popular than the Ogg container format, because many browser vendors are heavily pushing it as the open video format made for the web. It is also worth noting that WebM is being developed alongside an image format called WebP.

<video>

The video element (`<video>`) is implemented in a similar way to `<audio>`. As with `<audio>` you can specify either just one video file, or specify many using `<source>`:

```
<video>
    <source src='../video.ogv' type='video/ogg;'>
    <source src='../video.mp4' type='video/mp4'>
    <source src='../video.webm' type='video/webm'>
</video>
```

Again, as with audio, the browsers have an algorithm to choose the source based on the capabilities of the browser and operating system. It is not a problem to have many sources, in any order. The three formats in the example: Ogg, MP4, and WebM, are the best supported at the time of writing.

Attributes and Properties

So, now we know how to implement audio and video on our HTML document, let's look at the attributes and properties available to these elements. There is a lot of overlap between the audio and video elements, most attributes work on both, so I will explain them together instead of in separate sections.

Controls

Okay, so we have audio on our page now—but we can do more. Currently the browser can choose a file to play, but we have no way to tell it to play. Its current state is useful when we want to use JavaScript to control the audio or video, but ideally it should have a media player. Most browsers have a built-in player that can be triggered simply by adding controls to the element. Like so:

```
<audio controls>
    <source src='audio.ogg' type='audio/ogg; codecs=vorbis'>
    <source src='audio.mp3' type='audio/mpeg'>
</audio>
```

Likewise we would use the following code for a video:

```
<video controls>
    <source src='../video.ogv' type='video/ogg;'>
    <source src='../video.mp4' type='video/mp4'>
    <source src='../video.webm' type='video/webm'>
</video>
```

If you run that in your browser you should now see a basic audio (or video) player. If you want to provide a customized player, to fit the style of your website, then you are probably best creating the DOM elements and styling them as you wish then hooking it up to an <audio>/<video> element that does not have controls enabled.

▓ **Note**   Some browsers use Shadow DOM so in theory you could style the default controls with CSS but, at the time of writing, each browser is very different and the Shadow DOM is still new. I would recommend checking `www.caniuse.com` to see the current implementation status across browsers.

Autoplay

Occasionally you may have a legitimate reason to want audio or video to autoplay. While this is usually frowned upon, it is simple to do. As with controls, you can just add the autoplay attribute to the element. You can also set this using JavaScript with `element.autoplay = true`, like so:

```
<audio autoplay>
    <source src='audio.ogg' type='audio/ogg; codecs=vorbis'>
    <source src='audio.mp3' type='audio/mpeg'>
</audio>
```

And for video it would work in much the same way:

```
<video autoplay>
    <source src='../video.ogv' type='video/ogg;'>
    <source src='../video.mp4' type='video/mp4'>
    <source src='../video.webm' type='video/webm'>
</video>
```

Preload

This is slightly less obvious than the previous two attributes, preload is used to attempt to load either the entire audio or video file or the metadata (such as duration) at page load; this is based on the value of the attribute. If preload is not set, then it is the choice of the browser (the default is usually metadata). That said, even if the attribute is set, it is only a hint and is used as the preferred choice for the browser to consider it based on a number of conditions that change between browsers.

There are three acceptable values for preload. These are

- **auto**: This gives priority to the browser, if it is appropriate to do so. For example, if the connectivity is good, then it may try to download the entire file. With preload set to auto, the `readyState` variable will increment from 0 (nothing downloaded) to 4 (will play without interruption), a fully preloaded file will have a 4 `readyState`.

- **metadata**: This is the most commonly used value because it is a kind of "happy medium." It basically lets the browser know that it would be great to know about the file, including the duration for instance, but that the entire file isn't needed until the user clicks play. With preload set to metadata, the `readyState` will be set to 1 (has metadata) once the metadata has downloaded and may move to 2 or 3 depending on how aggressive the fetching is.

- **none**: This reduces stress on the server by telling the browser that no information is needed until the user clicks play. Of course, as I said earlier, this is just a hint and so it may decide to give the metadata or entire file anyway.

The attribute works just like the other examples, for audio:

```
<audio preload='metadata'>
    <source src='audio.ogg' type='audio/ogg; codecs=vorbis'>
    <source src='audio.mp3' type='audio/mpeg'>
</audio>
```

And for video:

```
<video preload='metadata'>
    <source src='../video.ogv' type='video/ogg;'>
    <source src='../video.mp4' type='video/mp4'>
    <source src='../video.webm' type='video/webm'>
</video>
```

▨ **Note** This attribute is well supported in most browsers, except Presto-based Opera browsers, which use the old name of autobuffer.

Loop

This is an attribute that forces the audio or video file to loop back to the beginning once the file has completed playing. This can be either set as an attribute (straight to the HTML) or as a property (from JavaScript). Using loop as a property lets you check the current state (whether it is true or false).

```
<audio loop>
    <source src='audio.ogg' type='audio/ogg; codecs=vorbis'>
    <source src='audio.mp3' type='audio/mpeg'>
</audio>
```

You can do the same for video:

```
<video loop>
    <source src='../video.ogv' type='video/ogg;'>
    <source src='../video.mp4' type='video/mp4'>
    <source src='../video.webm' type='video/webm'>
</video>
```

Played

You will often want to know which parts of the media have been played, especially if you are creating a media player or perhaps an advertisement of some kind. Played is a property that can be used with JavaScript to get a TimeRanges object that has the start and end times of each portion of the track that has been played. For example, if I listened to the beginning for about 20 seconds, then calling ele.played.start(0) would give 0 because it is the beginning and ele.played.end(0) would give 20; the parameter is the index, so 0 would be the first portion listened and 1 would be the second. You can use ele.played.length to find the amount of separate portions listened to.

```
var ele = document.querySelector('audio');
function log()  {
  for (var i = 0; i < ele.played.length; i++)
  {
      console.log("Portion " + i);
      console.log("  Start: " + ele.played.start(i));
      console.log("  End: " + ele.played.end(i));
  }
}
```

To change this to work with video, you just need to select video instead of audio:

```
var ele = document.querySelector('video');
```

In this example, if you run log() from the console, then you will see each portion of the audio or video that you have played to with the start and end times in seconds. Aside from purely demonstration purposes or for debugging, the played property is useful in media players as a way for users to see parts they have already listened to.

Buffered

As with played, we are able to get a TimeRanges object for the portions of the file that have buffered. It helps to know the buffered portions of the file when making a media player (which we will be doing in a later chapter) where instead of using the **controls** attribute, we can instead create a custom control that shows the buffered areas of the audio file. Unlike played, buffered may have multiple indexes, for example if the user has moved the playhead.

```
var ele = document.querySelector('audio');
// Or: var ele = document.querySelector('video');

function log()  {
    for (var i = 0; i < ele.buffered.length; i++)
    {
      console.log("Portion " + i);
      console.log("  Start: " + ele.buffered.start(i));
      console.log("  End: " + ele.buffered.end(i));
    }
}
```

Duration

To find the length of the audio or video file we can use the duration property, which returns the duration in seconds. If the audio or video element is streaming a file, then the duration will be set as infinity (specifically, according to the spec, positive infinity) unless the streaming stops. In this case the duration will be returned as the amount of seconds of the length of what has been streamed. If the duration changes, such as in the case of the streaming, then the durationchange event is triggered, you can use an event listener to trigger styling or DOM changes to let the user know a file has stopped streaming.

```
var ele = document.querySelector('audio');
// Or: var ele = document.querySelector('video');
console.log(ele.duration);
```

Volume

The volume property can be used to both get and set the volume; it is controlled using a number between 0.0 and 1.0. By default the initial volume will be 1.0, which is the maximum that the browser will allow (not necessarily the maximum of the speakers). The volume is simply a setter/getter property, making it easy to get access and to modify the volume:

```
var ele = document.querySelector('audio');
// Or: var ele = document.querySelector('video');

var vol = 0.5; // The volume you want to set it to

console.log(ele.volume);

ele.volume = vol;

console.log(ele.volume);
```

Playback Rate

The playbackrate is the speed at which the audio/video is played. The original speed is 1.0 and the rate is the multiplication of the initial speed. For example, if you change the playbackrate to 0.5, then you get the audio or video played in slow motion. On the other hand, if you change the rate to 1.5, the audio or video would be fast-forwarded.

```
var ele = document.querySelector('audio');
// Or: var ele = document.querySelector('video');

function slowMotion() {
    ele.playbackrate = 0.5;
}

function fastForward() {
    ele.playbackrate = 1.5;
}
```

Network State

This property is used to determine the network activity. It returns 4 numbers, from 0 to 3, which correspond to the following states:

- 0. NETWORK_EMPTY – This means that the element has not yet been initialized.
- 1. NETWORK_IDLE – This means that the correct audio/video file has been chosen, but is not currently using the network.
- 2. NETWORK_LOADING – The audio/video is being downloaded.
- 3. NETWORK_NO_SOURCE - Either none of the given files are compatible or no file was provided.

Unlike many of the previous properties, `networkState` is a read-only property. This code shows how it can be used:

```
var ele = document.querySelector('audio');
// Or: var ele = document.querySelector('video');

function logNetworkState()  {
    console.log(ele.networkState);
}
```

Web Audio API

Let's move on and delve into the realm of audio analysis, which we will be using in later chapters to create visualizations of the audio. For this we'll be using the Web Audio API.

The API is based on the concept of nodes, where each one takes the current audio (which could be either the original version or already have been through any number of nodes), which it then does something with. I said "something" to be purposely vague, nodes can be coded in any way that you want them to be. Some of the default usages include: channel splitting and merging, oscillation, and gain control. One analogy that I particularly like was one Stuart Memo made in his "An introduction to the Web Audio API" article in which he explained how the API nodes work just the same as adding a distortion pedal and an amp to a guitar, you can remove either node or add new nodes without having to do anything other than change the cables. For now, we are just going to use `AnalyserNode` to see exactly what is going on within the audio. From there we will start using other nodes to understand what has changed.

Analyzing Audio

First, we need to create both an audio context and an analyzer that we then connect together. The context is the interface that gives access to all properties of the audio, as well as the methods that are used to create and connect nodes.

```
var ele = document.querySelector('audio');
var ctx = new AudioContext();
var analyser = ctx.createAnalyser();

var source = ctx.createMediaElementSource(ele);
source.connect(analyser);
analyser.connect(ctx.destination);
```

You will note that I am using `createMediaElementSource` within a "source" variable. This simply re-routes the audio from the `<audio>` element into the API. This means that the audio you play through the element will now be controlled by and used as a node of the API's context graph (the way in which each node is connected). It also means that the Web Audio API, rather than the element, is controlling volume and other attributes (except controlling when the music is playing) so if you would still like to use the element controls, you need to hook it up using a GainNode, like so:

```
var ele = document.querySelector('audio');
var ctx = new AudioContext();
var analyser = ctx.createAnalyser();
```

```
var source = ctx.createMediaElementSource(ele);
var volumeControl = ctx.createGainNode();
source.connect(volumeControl);
volumeControl.connect(analyser);
analyser.connect(ctx.destination);

ele.addEventListener('onvolumechange', volumeControl, false);

function volumeChange()  {
    volumeControl.gain.value = ele.volume;
}

function log()  {
    freqData = new Uint8Array(analyser.frequencyBinCount);
    analyser.getByteFrequencyData(freqData);
    console.log(freqData);
}
```

░ **Note**   At the time of writing, the onvolumechange event does not work as a dynamic event listener, so instead you need to include onvolumechange="volumeChange();" on the <audio> element.

Now back to the analyzer. This node gives us access to data from a Fast Fourier Transform (FFT), which is a complicated algorithm used for a variety of things including audio analysis. There are two types of data available, frequency and time domain. Frequency data can be gained using getFloatFrequencyData or getByteFrequencyData (depending on type of data you want, we will be using the second to store the data in an array of bytes) both of these methods give an array of normalized frequencies. The reason for the two methods is that the resolution (that is, the quality) of the float array is much higher than that of the byte. Due to the way it is normalized, we need to go through each index of the array and multiply it by the sample rate divided by size of the FFT. To see the outcome of this, let's log it to the console:

```
function log()  {
    freqData = new Uint8Array(analyser.frequencyBinCount);
    analyser.getByteFrequencyData(freqData);
    for (var i = 0; i < freqData.length; i++) {
        console.log(freqData[i] * ctx.sampleRate / analyser.fftSize);
    }
}
```

You should now see a variety of numbers, which are dependent on the audio you are playing. Each number represents the frequency (440Hz is the easiest frequency to remember, this is the A above Middle C), which we will go into more detail in a later chapter (where I introduce some music theory). For now, just look at the data and think of things you can do with it (maybe even try to implement them). Of course, a list of seemingly random numbers is no good to anyone, visualizations are key to understanding any type of data, and so we are now going to use what we learned in the previous chapter to create 2D graphs that visualize the music.

Frequency Visualization

We could spend the entire book making fun games or random animations that look great but are not too useful; instead, let's look at the kind of tools we can make when we use the Web Audio API and canvas together. This example will be frequency visualization, and the next will be a spectrogram. To start with, let's use the original output of getByteFrequencyData to produce a simple bar chart style visualization of the normalized frequencies (this makes it easy to chart, due to the 255 cap). To do this we need to set up variables for references to the audio and canvas elements, as well as the contexts for each and an analyzer node. I would also recommend setting up the volume control as we did earlier, so that you can see how the visualization changes dependent on the volume (as well as just so that you can easily turn it down!), I find it quite interesting. For the nodes, we need to connect the source to the volume which is then connected to the analyzer before output to the speakers (destination).

```
var audioEle = document.querySelector('audio');
var audioCtx = new AudioContext();
var canvasEle = document.querySelector('canvas');
var canvasCtx = canvasEle.getContext('2d');

var analyser = audioCtx.createAnalyser();

var source = audioCtx.createMediaElementSource(audioEle);
var volumeControl = audioCtx.createGainNode();

source.connect(volumeControl);
volumeControl.connect(analyser);
analyser.connect(audioCtx.destination);
```

Now we need to add, alongside the volumeChange function we used earlier, both logic and draw functions. Within logic we simply need to grab the frequency data and send it over to the draw function where it will draw it to the canvas. I think it looks good with thin lines for the visualization but you can change that by modifying the x position (I chose i, for current frequency, meaning they are all next to each other) and the width (which I kept as 1 to keep thin). Of course you need to remember to call logic, I have used setInterval for this.

```
function volumeChange()  {
    volumeControl.gain.value = audioEle.volume;
}

function logic()  {
    var freqData = new Uint8Array(analyser.frequencyBinCount);
    analyser.getByteFrequencyData(freqData);
    requestAnimationFrame(function() {
        draw(freqData);
    });
}

function draw(freqData)  {
    canvasCtx.clearRect(0, 0, canvasEle.width, canvasEle.height);
    canvasCtx.fillStyle = "#ff0000";
    for (var i = 0; i < freqData.length; i++) {
        canvasCtx.fillRect(i, canvasEle.height, 1, canvasEle.height - freqData[i]);
    }
}

setInterval(logic, 1000/60);
```

Figure 3-1 shows the outcome of the frequency visualization while the audio is playing.

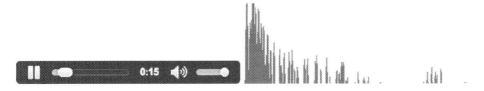

Figure 3-1. *This shows the frequency visualization*

▓ **Note**   You may see a wall of red; this is probably due to the volume being muted. Turn up the volume to get the correct visualization.

This should all be very self-explanatory, as we have already gone through each of these concepts, such as audio processing nodes and canvas drawing. You can find the code in Listing 3-1 as well as in the files that accompany this book.

Listing 3-1. Code for the Frequency Visualization

```html
<!DOCTYPE html>
<html>
    <head>
        <title>Chapter 3 - Frequency Visualisation</title>
    </head>

    <body>
        <audio controls onvolumechange="volumeChange();">
                <source src='../audio.ogg' type='audio/ogg; codecs=vorbis'>
                    <source src='../audio.mp3' type='audio/mpeg'>
        </audio>
        <canvas>Canvas is not supported by your browser</canvas>
        <script src="script.js"></script>
    </body>
</html>

// Pollyfill for AudioContext
(function() {
    window.AudioContext = window.AudioContext || window.webkitAudioContext;
  var requestAnimationFrame = window.requestAnimationFrame || window.mozRequestAnimationFrame ||
                        window.webkitRequestAnimationFrame || window.msRequestAnimationFrame;
  window.requestAnimationFrame = requestAnimationFrame;
})();

var audioEle = document.querySelector('audio');
var audioCtx = new AudioContext();
var canvasEle = document.querySelector('canvas');
var canvasCtx = canvasEle.getContext('2d');
```

```
var analyser = audioCtx.createAnalyser();

var source = audioCtx.createMediaElementSource(audioEle);
var volumeControl = audioCtx.createGainNode();

source.connect(volumeControl);
volumeControl.connect(analyser);
analyser.connect(audioCtx.destination);

//audioEle.addEventListener('onvolumechange', volumeControl, false);

function volumeChange()  {
    volumeControl.gain.value = audioEle.volume;
}

function logic()  {
    var freqData = new Uint8Array(analyser.frequencyBinCount);
    analyser.getByteFrequencyData(freqData);
    requestAnimationFrame(function() {
        draw(freqData);
    });
}

function draw(freqData)  {
    canvasCtx.clearRect(0, 0, canvasEle.width, canvasEle.height);
    canvasCtx.fillStyle = "#ff0000";
    for (var i = 0; i < freqData.length; i++) {
        canvasCtx.fillRect(i, canvasEle.height, 1, canvasEle.height - freqData[i]);
    }
}

setInterval(logic, 1000/60);
```

Spectrogram

With our previous visualization you can easily see the frequencies and the way the audio changes, but only at any given time. Now we are going to use a spectrogram, which shows how the audio changes over time, where the x axis is time, y is part of the audio, and the color is frequency. This is used for a number of things from simply nice patterns to speech recognition. Because a spectrogram is similar to the previous visualization, with the extra dimension of time, we might as well work from our existing code. One event that I would like to now introduce is onaudioprocess. The event is part of a JavaScriptNode, created using the following line:

```
var logger = audioCtx.createJavaScriptNode(analyser.frequencyBinCount, 1, 1);
```

The onaudioprocess event works at the same speed as the audio is playing, allowing it to be the perfect replacement to setInterval for audio logic (in the same way we use requestAnimationFrame to render at a more accurate and dynamic speed for animation Let's also create a variable called x that will hold the current position in time, so that we know how many iterations to draw until we hit the current position.

```
var logger = audioCtx.createJavaScriptNode(analyser.frequencyBinCount, 1, 1);
logger.onaudioprocess = function () {
    logic();
}
```

```
var x = 0;

function logic()  {
    if(!audioEle.paused)  {
        x += 1;
        var freqData = new Uint8Array(analyser.frequencyBinCount);
        analyser.getByteFrequencyData(freqData);
        requestAnimationFrame(function() {
            draw(freqData);
        });
    }
}
```

Here is the code for that, you can see that it is very similar to our early code except that it uses onaudioprocess and checks that the element is not paused. Both of these are improvements you could make to our previous code; I just didn't want to chuck everything in at once. We now just need to draw our visualization! But where to start? Simple—we start with trying to work out what we are doing. In this case, we want to draw individual columns where each pixel represents the frequency (normalized) as a color. To do this we will be using HSL instead of RGB, because it allows us to set the hue as a number between 0 and 255 (which is exactly what we get from getByteFrequencyData) rather than requiring each color to be specified. Once it has drawn even column on the canvas, I will be clearing it and carrying on from the beginning as if turning a new page, you may want to improve this by sliding rather than clearing.

```
function draw(freqData)  {
    if (x > canvasEle.width)  {
        canvasCtx.clearRect(0, 0, canvasEle.width, canvasEle.height);
        x = 0;
    }

    for (var i = 0; i < freqData.length; i++) {
        canvasCtx.fillStyle = "hsl(" + freqData[i] + ",100%, 50%)";
        canvasCtx.fillRect(x, canvasEle.height - i, 1, 1);
    }
}
```

You should now understand how we can take the frequency data and produce a variety of visualizations, and they don't have to be just purely decorative either. Figure 3-2 shows how the spectrogram looks after some audio has been played. As always, the full code can be found in the download that accompanies this book.

Figure 3-2. *This shows the spectrogram*

■ **Note**   As with the previous example, you may see a wall of red; this is probably due to the volume being muted. Turn up the volume to get the correct visualization.

Listing 3-2 shows the complete code required for the Spectrogram, it can also be found in the download for the book.

Listing 3-2. Code for the Spectrogram

```html
<!DOCTYPE html>
<html>
    <head>
        <title>Chapter 3 - Spectrogram</title>
    </head>

    <body>
        <audio controls onvolumechange="volumeChange();">
            <source src='../audio.ogg' type='audio/ogg; codecs=vorbis'>
              <source src='../audio.mp3' type='audio/mpeg'>
        </audio>
        <canvas>Canvas is not supported by your browser</canvas>
        <script src="script.js"></script>
    </body>
</html>
```

```javascript
// Pollyfill for AudioContext
(function() {
    window.AudioContext = window.AudioContext || window.webkitAudioContext || window.
mozAudioContext;
  var requestAnimationFrame = window.requestAnimationFrame || window.mozRequestAnimationFrame ||
                        window.webkitRequestAnimationFrame || window.msRequestAnimationFrame;
  window.requestAnimationFrame = requestAnimationFrame;
})();

var audioEle = document.querySelector('audio');
var audioCtx = new AudioContext();
var canvasEle = document.querySelector('canvas');
var canvasCtx = canvasEle.getContext('2d');

var analyser = audioCtx.createAnalyser();
analyser.smoothingTimeConstant = 0;

var logger = audioCtx.createJavaScriptNode(analyser.frequencyBinCount, 1, 1);

var source = audioCtx.createMediaElementSource(audioEle);
var volumeControl = audioCtx.createGainNode();

source.connect(volumeControl);
volumeControl.connect(analyser);
analyser.connect(audioCtx.destination);
logger.connect(audioCtx.destination);
```

```
//audioEle.addEventListener('onvolumechange', volumeControl, false);

logger.onaudioprocess = function () {
    logic();
}

function volumeChange()  {
    volumeControl.gain.value = audioEle.volume;
}

var x = 0;

function logic()  {
    if(!audioEle.paused)  {
        x += 1;
        var freqData = new Uint8Array(analyser.frequencyBinCount);
        analyser.getByteFrequencyData(freqData);
        requestAnimationFrame(function() {
            draw(freqData);
        });
    }
}

function draw(freqData)  {
    if (x > canvasEle.width)  {
        canvasCtx.clearRect(0, 0, canvasEle.width, canvasEle.height);
        x = 0;
    }

    for (var i = 0; i < freqData.length; i++) {
        canvasCtx.fillStyle = "hsl(" + freqData[i] + ",100%, 50%)";
        canvasCtx.fillRect(x, canvasEle.height - i, 1, 1);
    }
}
```

Web Audio API Nodes

We have used a few Web Audio API nodes already such as MediaElementSource, GainNode, and Analyser. Here is an overview of the other nodes and methods available.

Name of Node	Description
AnalyserNode	Obtains data about the current state of audio, such as frequencies.
AudioBufferSourceNode	Buffers short audio assets to be used as temporary but easy to access storage.
BiquadFilterNode	Processes basic filters (known as low-level filters), such as low/high pass, where frequencies are cutoff either below or above the given value.
ChannelSplitterNode	Splits each channel so that you can use them within the process graph separately for a finer control.

(*continued*)

Name of Node	Description
ChannelMergerNode	Merges any channels that have been split (or otherwise need merging) using this merger node.
ConvolverNode	Applies a linear convolution effect, which is how sound can be manipulated to simulate acoustic space or a high-quality effect.
DelayNode	Delays the output (to the next node in the process graph) by a specific amount of time.
GainNode	Changes the volume of audio by multiplying the audio by the gain attribute.
MediaElementAudioSourceNode	Allows you to connect a media element to the Web Audio API.
PannerNode	Specializes sound in a 3d space. This is usually used heavily within games, but may be useful elsewhere too.
WaveShaperNode	Used for non-linear distortion.

Manipulating Video

Unfortunately, there is no API like the Web Audio API that is used for video so you need to manipulate the video yourself. Of course, analyzing the video in the same way as analyzing the audio would be far harder than using the Web Audio API. However, it is not terribly hard to create a basic filter. I am going to go through a simple invert filter, so that we do not get bogged down in the math. We will not go past simple filters in this chapter because Chapters 9 and 10 will extend this chapter by using object detection on real-time video as an input for controlling the keyboard that we will create in Chapter 5.

The principle of invert is that we go through each pixel and invert it, by subtracting the current value of a color from 255. The output of this gets drawn onto a canvas, which is shown. For this example I will be showing the canvas alongside the video element, but you may prefer to hide the video element altogether.

Note You may need to run this on a server (or localhost) due to Cross-Origin Resource Sharing policies.

We start as usual, by setting up the variables for elements and contexts. Once that is complete we can start on the function for manipulating the video source. First, you need to draw the current frame of the video onto the canvas.

```
var canvasEle = document.querySelector('canvas');
var canvasCtx = canvasEle.getContext('2d');

var videoEle = document.querySelector('video');
var w = videoEle.clientWidth;
var h = videoEle.clientHeight;

canvasEle.width = w;
canvasEle.height = h;
```

We then need to get the image data and iterate over it, for each pixel (remember, each pixel is made out of 4 separate values for RGBA. We flip them by subtracting the current value from 255, as I previously explained. Once that is done, we can put the image data back and then use requestAnimationFrame to call the draw function again.

```
drawInvertedFrame();

function drawInvertedFrame()  {
    canvasCtx.drawImage(videoEle, 0, 0, w, h);
    var manip = canvasCtx.getImageData(0, 0, w, h);
    var data = manip.data;

    // Iterate through each pixel, inverting it
    for (var i = 0; i < data.length; i += 4) {
        var r = data[i],
            g = data[i+1],
            b = data[i+2];
        data[i] = 255 - r;
        data[i+1] = 255 - g;
        data[i+2] = 255 - b;
    }

    canvasCtx.putImageData(manip, 0, 0);

    requestAnimationFrame(drawInvertedFrame);
}
```

The following image, Figure 3-3, shows the inverted video being rendered in real-time alongside the original video.

Figure 3-3. *This figure shows the invert filter on a video alongside the original*

As always, the complete code listing for this is available in the downloadable file that complements this book.

Summary

This chapter allowed you to explore audio and video on the web. You should now have a solid understanding of the different codecs that you can use, with the advantages and disadvantages of each. I have tried also to delve into Web Audio API quite deeply. I hope that by linking it into the previous chapter using visualizations rather than just giving you a large amount of numbers, that you can understand it and find it much more useful.

I would like to encourage you to play around with the Web Audio API as well as to try video manipulation—there are a lot of very interesting effects that you can create that you may find useful (especially as a visual aide and for nice details) within general web design and development. Aside from simple websites, there is a lot of room for more of a web app kind of thing, such as the media player we will soon be creating.

CHAPTER 4

Beginning 3D

Before we start creating the media player, I would like to spend a chapter going through 3D from basic shapes to visualizations. In the upcoming chapters we will be creating music visualizations as part of the media player but you should feel comfortable with all kinds of usages of 3D, especially data visualizations. To begin with let's take a look at 3D graphics in general, before moving on to using a library called Three.js. Much of the basics will be familiar to you, but I would like to start from the beginning to make sure I cover it fully.

Basics of 3D

As you know, a 3D world (much like our own) consists of three dimensions: x, y, and z. These dimensions can be visualized simply by thinking of a standard Cartesian graph, where you have an axis pointing right for x, another pointing up representing y, and a third that shows depth, which is the z-axis. I say that z represents depth, because that is how it feels, but actually positive z comes toward you while negative goes away. You can see an example of this in Figure 4-1.

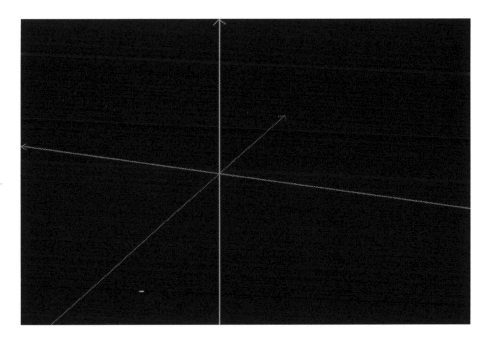

Figure 4-1. *3D axes*

In the 3D world, objects and shapes are created using meshes. A *mesh* could be as complicated as you like, from a simple cube to an object that you have designed using 3D modeling software (we will not be going that far, but I will explain how to import the models). To give an appearance to a mesh you can use materials, which is similar to the real world in that each material has its own set of properties, such as color and opacity. We will take a look at defining our own materials later in the chapter.

As well as meshes and materials, we also have camera and lights. Whereas in a 2D animation we often move the shapes around, in a 3D animation we have the option of moving the camera (that is, what the user can see) around the scene. I mentioned lights and it is obvious what these are for, but you may well be surprised at how many different types of lighting there are. Lighting and cameras each have their own sections later in this chapter. It can be rather impressive seeing how a scene can be changed just by changing the type or position of the lights.

Three.js

Three.js is a library that makes it much easier to render 3D within the browser. It allows you to use a number of renderers, including canvas and WebGL. I would usually recommend avoiding libraries but to use WebGL without a library you need to write shaders (which are required to use WebGL due to the reliance on a GPU) in a language called GLSL, which has syntax similar to C. Learning GLSL is overkill for the aims of this book and would take longer than one chapter! I will be using version 56 of Three.js, which is also included in the downloadable source code, but you can find the latest version at `http://www.mrdoob.github.com/three.js/`.

Make a Scene

You can think of a scene in the same way as you would in a film–it is where you put the meshes (objects), lighting, and cameras. The scene is your stage. You can set up a scene quite simply, as all you require is the scene itself, a camera, and the renderer. Of course, that would be an empty scene! A simple scene object can be created using `THREE.Scene()` so let's go ahead and create a basic (empty) scene. Afterward we can start adding basic geometry such as cubes or spheres.

We can start by creating variables for width and height to store the size of the renderer (that is, our viewport) so for this example I am going to set each to use the dimensions of the inner window. We also need a container to put the renderer in, unlike previous chapters where we made a canvas ourselves; we can let Three.js create the DOM, depending on the renderer we choose. Now we need to choose the renderer, Three.js is built in such a way that you can create your own renderer or use a third-party's renderer but the only ones you really need to know about are the `CanvasRenderer` and `WebGLRenderer`. The difference between these is that canvas is more widely supported but WebGL is more efficient. This is because WebGL has native 3D support (OpenGL ES 2) in which the 3D math runs on the GPU, whereas Canvas has no 3D support (you have to write it yourself) meaning its 3D math runs in JavaScript (much slower). So let's just stick to using WebGLRenderer for now, you might want to try both though just to get a feel for the differences (they are usually only subtle). With the renderer chosen, I have stored it in a variable called `renderer`, we can set the dimensions and add it to the DOM.

```
var width  = window.innerWidth,
height = window.innerHeight;

var container = document.querySelector('#container');

var renderer = new THREE.WebGLRenderer();
renderer.setSize(width, height);
container.appendChild(renderer.domElement);
```

From here we need to create a camera. Later in the chapter I will go through how to use multiple cameras, but to start with let's just have one. As with renderers, there are a couple of default camera classes and it is very easy to code your own type of camera by inheriting from the abstract `Camera` class. The built-in cameras are `OrthographicCamera` and PerspectiveCamera, which we can use to provide different views of the scene; you can usually consider perspective as showing a 3D view, while orthographic shows a 2D view. For this example let's choose the perspective because we just want to see what is on the scene (which to start with will be nothing) rather than a particular view (such as top down). For our PerspectiveCamera there are four parameters, which according to the documentation are

- **fov**: Camera frustum vertical field of view
- **aspect**: Camera frustum aspect ratio
- **near**: Camera frustum near plane
- **far**: Camera frustum far plane

This makes sense providing you know the meaning of frustum; in this case it is simply the portion of the view. Often these parameters are stored as variables but since we have no use for them elsewhere at the moment, I have decided to write the values directly as parameters to reduce the amount of lines of code. With a camera created we can position it, for now let's just set the camera's z dimension to 300 so that the scene is nicely in view once we add some meshes.

```
var camera = new THREE.PerspectiveCamera(45, width / height, 1, 1000);
camera.position.z = 300;
```

Once we have objects in the scene, you will probably benefit from fiddling with these numbers to get a feel for how they affect the view of the scene. As I mentioned earlier, to create the scene itself all you need to do is create an instance of the Scene class. With the scene created, we can add the camera to it. To render the scene we use renderer.render(scene, camera); which is self-explanatory have decided to put this within a similar set up to the one we used in Chapter 2.This works very nicely as a boilerplate for developing more advanced animations and renders.

```
var scene = new THREE.Scene();
scene.add(camera);

function logic() {
    requestAnimationFrame(render);
}

function render() {
    renderer.render(scene, camera);
}

setInterval(logic, 1000/60);
```

Adding Meshes

A basic scene is rather boring and, quite frankly, useless. So let's spice things up a bit by taking a look at the kinds of meshes we can use. Firstly though, we need some lighting so that we can actually see the objects (it really is like being in a room in the dark–the objects are on the scene but you cannot see them). I will explain the types of lights shortly, but for now we can just use a simple DirectionalLight, which is used just like a desk lamp in that it points in a specific direction rather than covering the entire scene. I chose to use this type of lighting because it allows us to easily see shadows straight away. A default directional light is white and has an intensity of 1; by default the light points toward the center to the scene (0,0,0). It should be noted that although the directional light has a property called position, that is the direction that the light is pointed and the light source itself does not have an actual position (it is infinite). I have decided to place light further toward the camera, so that we can see a nice simple shadow around the object.

```
var directionalLight = new THREE.DirectionalLight();
directionalLight.position.z = 10;
scene.add(directionalLight);
```

Let's start with a sphere (similar to that of the official documentation for Three.js). To create any primitive object, we need to create a mesh that includes the type of geometry and the material. For a sphere we can use THREE.SphereGeometry with any type of material, in this example I will be using a material called THREE.MeshLambertMaterial (more information about that soon).

```
var radius = 100,
    segments = 50,
    rings = 50;

var sphereMaterial = new THREE.MeshLambertMaterial(
{
  color: 0xFF0000
});

var sphere = new THREE.Mesh(
    new THREE.SphereGeometry(
        radius,
        segments,
        rings),
    sphereMaterial);
scene.add(sphere);
```

As you can see, I have started by setting up three variables to control the properties of the sphere. You will know that radius is half of the size/diameter of the sphere. Segments and rings are used to specify the quality of the sphere– the lower the numbers the lower quality. Try changing them from 50 to 10, you will see jagged edges and will probably be able to see where the lines are that make up the rings and segments. You can think of them similar to latitude and longitude; rings go horizontally around the sphere and segments are vertical.

░ **Note**   If you are familiar with bitmap images or mathematical geometry, you will understand that there is no perfect curve, so there is no correct answer for how many rings and segments you should have. Just choose the number that feels right as a tradeoff between quality and optimization.

If you run the following code you should see a red sphere.

```
<!DOCTYPE html>
<html>
  <head>
    <title>Shapes In Scene</title>
    <style>
      * { margin: 0; }
      canvas { background: #000;}
    </style>
  </head>
  <body>
    <div id="container"></div>
```

```
      <script src="../three.min.js"></script>
      <script src="script.js"></script>
   </body>
</html>
var width  = window.innerWidth,
height = window.innerHeight;

var container = document.querySelector('#container');

var renderer = new THREE.WebGLRenderer();
renderer.setSize(width, height);
container.appendChild(renderer.domElement);

var VIEW_ANGLE = 45,
    NEAR = 0.1,
    FAR = 10000;
var camera =  new THREE.PerspectiveCamera(45, width / height, 1, 1000);
camera.position.z = 300;

var scene = new THREE.Scene();
scene.add(camera);

var directionalLight = new THREE.DirectionalLight();
directionalLight.position.z = 10;
scene.add(directionalLight);

var radius = 100,
    segments = 50,
    rings = 50;

var sphereMaterial = new THREE.MeshLambertMaterial(
{
  color: 0xFF0000
});

var sphere = new THREE.Mesh(
    new THREE.SphereGeometry(
        radius,
        segments,
        rings),
    sphereMaterial);
scene.add(sphere);

function logic()  {
  requestAnimationFrame(render);
}

function render() {
  renderer.render(scene, camera);
}

setInterval(logic, 1000/60);
```

59

Creating each primitive shape is similar so instead of guiding you through each shape, here is a Table 4-1 shows the types of shapes. Do note that unless I specify otherwise, every parameter of the constructor is optional. Many of the geometries are based on PolyhedronGeometry, so the parameter detail is used to determine the amount of triangles are used to create the shape. Also remember that all constructors should be prepended with THREE.

Table 4-1. *Showing geometries avaiable in Three.js*

Name	Constructor	Notes
CircleGeometry	CircleGeometry (radius, segments, thetaStart, thetaLength)	The theta parameters are used to create segments; by changing them you can specify a particular arc.
ConvexGeometry	ConvexGeometry (vertices)	
CubeGeometry	CubeGeometry (width, height, depth, widthSegments, heightSegments, depthSegment)	
CylinderGeometry	CylinderGeometry (radiusTop, radiusBottom, height, radiusSegments, heightSegments, openEnded)	
ExtrudeGeometry	ExtrudeGeometry (shapes, options)	There are many options for this one so I will go through them after this table.
IcosahedronGeometry	IcosahedronGeometry (radius, detail)	
LatheGeometry	LatheGeometry (points, segments, phiStart, phiLength)	
OctahedronGeometry	OctahedronGeometry (radius, detail)	
ParametricGeometry	ParametricGeometry (parametricFunction, uSegments, ySegments, useTris)	
PlaneGeometry	PlaneGeometry (width, height, widthSegments, heightSegments)	
PolyhedronGeometry	PolyhedronGeometry (vertices, faces, radius, detail)	
RingGeometry	RingGeometry (innerRadius, outerRadius, thetaSegments, phiSegments, thetaStart, thetaLength)	
ShapeGeometry	ShapeGeometry (shapes, options)	
SphereGeometry	SphereGeometry (radius, widthSegments, heightSegments, phiStart, phiLength, thetaStart, thetaLength)	We have already been through spheres, but as with circles there are some extra options that may be useful occasionally.

(continued)

Table 4-1. (*continued*)

Name	Constructor	Notes
TetrahedronGeometry	TetrahedronGeometry (radius, detail)	
TextGeometry	TextGeometry (text, parameters)	This is used to create 3D text, which I will go over later in the chapter.
TorusGeometry	TorusGeometry (radius, tube, radialSegments, tubularSegments, arc)	
TorusKnotGeometry	TorusKnotGeometry (radius, tube, radialSegments, tubularSegments, p, q, heightScale)	
TubeGeometry	TubeGeometry (path, segments, radius, radiusSegments, closed, debug)	

Extrusion

Most of these shapes will make sense to you; however ExtrudeGeometry is used differently and has many options. The purpose is to extend a shape, such as turning a 2D shape into 3D or building on one of the faces of a 3D shape. For this example we are going to start with some points as a path, which represent a basic 2D right-angled triangle, from which we will produce a 2D shape (that is, a plane created from the points in the path). With the shape created, we then need to extrude it to make into a prism.

░ **Note**　I have used a triangle for simplicity. Paths are usually used to create complex shapes.

The *path* is an array of points that are created using 2D vectors (which represent the coordinates of a graph). Three.js provides a useful library for dealing with vectors, which makes it very simple to work out the distance between two points and similar functions. To turn the path into a shape, you can just pass the path to the THREE.Shape constructor as a parameter.

```
var path = [];
path.push( new THREE.Vector2 (   0,  50 ) );
path.push( new THREE.Vector2 (  50,  50 ) );
path.push( new THREE.Vector2 (  50,   0 ) );
var shape = new THREE.Shape( path );
```

As I mentioned earlier, ExtrudeGeometry has a lot of options for defining the type of extrusion that is needed as seen in Table 4-2.

Table 4-2. *Showing the options avaiable for* ExtrudeGeometry

curveSegments	The number of points on the path, 12 by default.
steps	The amount of subdivisions within every extrusion. This defaults to 32.
amount	This is the amount of extrusions to make, basically the size of the shape, defaults to 100.
bevelEnabled	Enables bevel, which rounds the vertices that connect the edges of the extrusion to the faces of the shape. This is (true) by default.
bevelThickness	The thickness of the bevel, defaults to 6.
bevelSize	This is the distance from the edge that the bevel starts. It defaults to bevelThickness minus 2.
bevelSegments	The amount of segments of the bevel, similar to that of spheres in that it controls the quality of the bevel. Defaults to 3.
extrudePath	A particular path within the shape that should be extruded.
frames	This is an array of Frenet frames that expose the tangents, normal, and binormals of the spline. This is out of the scope of the book, but it defaults to generating the frames itself.
material	This is the material index for the front and back faces, it has no default.
extrudeMaterial	This is the material index for the extruded faces, it has no default.
uvGenerator	This allows you to specify the UV generator. By default it uses THREE.ExtrudeGeometry. WorldUVGenerator.

■ **Note** These options are subject to change, especially the defaults, between versions of the library.

The code that follows creates an extruded geometry to show how the various settings can be used to produce a fairly complicated shape.

```
var extrusionSettings = {
  size: 30, height: 4, curveSegments: 3,
  bevelThickness: 1, bevelSize: 2, bevelEnabled: false,
  material: 0, extrudeMaterial: 1
};

var extrude = new THREE.ExtrudeGeometry( shape, extrusionSettings );
var extrudedShape = new THREE.Mesh( extrude, material );
scene.add(extrudedShape);
```

Now, you may look at this code, see what appears on your screen, and be a bit confused. It is meant to look like a triangle, don't worry! It looks like that due to the viewpoint of the camera, so let's make the shape rotate so that you can see it in all its 3D goodness. I quite like the effect of rotating on the x and y axes. It kind of gives a figure-eight motion, which is useful for seeing all sides of the shape. This code adds rotation to the shape:

```
function logic() {
    extrudedShape.rotation.y += 0.05;
    extrudedShape.rotation.x += 0.05;
    requestAnimationFrame(render);
}
```

Figure 4-2 shows the extruded shape with the added rotation.

Figure 4-2. *Extrusion*

Text

There may be times when you need 3D text. It is not a common use case, but perhaps you are making something that feels like the titles of a movie or an advertisement. It is also something that many people do not realize is easily possible, so I would like to briefly take a look at it. The TextGeometry builds on the ExtrusionGeometry so it will be mostly familiar. Let's create 3D text that says "Hello World!"–because everyone loves Hello World–that rotates in the same shape as our prism did to show how similar they are (and because I find the rotation very mesmerizing to look at).

▩ **Caution** By default, Three.js uses a font called Helvetiker (it is not a spelling mistake) that must be included or you should use a different font, otherwise there will be errors. This font can be downloaded from http://www.typeface.neocracy.org/ and is also included in the source code for this book.

I am modifying the code we used for extrusion, so will be reusing the lighting and materials as well as the rest of the set up code. TextGeometry is no different than any other geometry, so it needs to be passed to a Mesh before it can be added to the scene; this probably seems obvious but I keep forgetting! Let's start with the default text:

```
var text = new THREE.Mesh(new THREE.TextGeometry("Hello World!", {}), material);
scene.add(text);
```

There are a number of other options that we can use to customize the text as shown in Table 4-3.

Table 4-3. *Showing the options avaiable for* TextGeometry

size	The size of the text, defaults to 150.
height	The thickness of the extruded text. The default is 50.
curveSegments	The number of points on the curve, defaults to 12.
font	The name of the font. The default is Helvetiker.
weight	This is the font weight. It can be any valid CSS font-weight, such as normal and bold. The default is normal.
style	As with weight, style allows any valid CSS font-style, such as normal and italic. The default is normal.
bevelEnabled	Enables bevel, which rounds the vertices that connect the edges of the extrusion to the faces of the shape. This is false by default.
bevelThickness	The thickness of the bevel, defaults to 6.
bevelSize	This is the distance from the edge that the bevel starts; it defaults to bevelThickness minus 2.

These options should be easy to understand because they are mostly from the CSS font options or from ExtrudedGeometry that we have already discussed. I will however show you a quick example of how these options can be used:

```
var options = {
  size: 20,
  height: 20,
  bevelEnabled: true,
  bevelThickness: 25
};

var text = new THREE.Mesh(new THREE.TextGeometry("Hello World!", options), material);
scene.add(text);
```

As you can see, it is quite easy to add text if you think of it as just another shape.

Lighting

Lighting is the one thing that I find really "sets the scene" (if you will pardon my pun) because the entire scene depends on the lighting for what will show (and what will be shadows, which is equally important) as well as the general ambience. Just like in a film, lighting can be used to completely change how the user feels. I will not get into user experience design, but it is worth remembering and thinking about!

▧ **Note** Because the lighting is dependent on the material of the object, you need to make sure the material is set up correctly. This will be explained in the next section, but for now make sure to use either MeshLambertMaterial or MeshPongMaterial because they are set up to work with lights.

I am going to go through some of the more commonly used types of lighting; of course there are others and you can create your own, some of which we may touch on briefly later. Each type of light has a number of properties and parameters, though some have more than others, here are a few that you should be familiar with:

- **Intensity**: The intensity of a light is how bright it is, the number can range from 0 to 1, where 1 is the actual color of the light and 0 is invisible (as if it is turned off). The default is usually 1. Some lights do not have intensity (at least at the time of writing) but you can always mimic it by multiplying each RGB color by an intensity variable.

- **Hex**: This is a color that must be in the form of hex (such as white being 0xffffff). Usually this defaults to white.

- **Shadows**: There are quite a few properties about shadows, such as whether the light casts shadows. I discuss these once I have explained each type of light.

Throughout the chapter we have been using a `DirectionalLight` as the only light source in the scene. As I explained earlier, a `DirectionalLight` is a light source that is cast in a particular direction and affects every object in that direction regardless of distance from the source. I should also remind you what I said earlier about `DirectionalLight` not having an actual position as such, instead the position that you set is the location from which it directs the light to the origin of the scene. The syntax for `DirectionalLight` is

```
THREE.DirectionalLight (hex, intensity)
```

A `PointLight` on the other hand emits light in all directions but the effect on the objects can differ depending on the distance from the source if a distance is set. When the distance is set to 0 (which it is by default), then the light will affect all objects like `DirectionalLight`s do. The syntax for `PointLight` is

```
THREE.PointLight (hex, intensity, distance)
```

There is another light, called a `SpotLight`, which can be used like a `DirectionalLight` but can be controlled much more precisely. One difference between `SpotLight` and `DirectionalLight` is angles. With a `DirectionalLight` the light emits in the general direction, whereas a `SpotLight` emits the light directionally within a specified angle (that defaults to pi/2). It also can cover a specified distance like the `PointLight`. You can usually use the other two lights if you want to just light a scene, but if you want to carefully direct the lighting, then this is the ideal light source. The syntax for `SpotLight` is

```
THREE.SpotLight (hex, intensity, distance, angle, exponent)
```

I mentioned about lighting causing an ambience. There is a light just for that called, as you might expect, `AmbientLight`. This light affects every object in the scene that can be affected by a light source. Because it is used to enhance the lighting, it should only be used with other lighting. The syntax for `AmbientLight` is

```
THREE.AmbientLight (hex)
```

You will probably find that the `AmbientLight` takes priority over all other lighting, and to fix that just change the intensity so that it is only a weak light (ambient). An example of changing intensity is

```
var light = new THREE.AmbientLight();
var intensity = 0.025;
scene.add(light);
light.color.setRGB( 20 * intensity, 0 * intensity, 255 * intensity );
```

Quite often you will want to know exactly what the lights are doing, where they are positioned, and the direction that the light is being cast. There are many ways to do this–you could use the console to look at the properties of each light but I would suggest something more graphical. For many of the lights, Three.js provides helper objects that show the direction using lines. If you have a DirectionalLight, then you can use a DirectionalLightHelper, which shows a dotted line in the direction it is pointing. You can change the type of line, such as color or dashes, by changing the material. Most of the lights also have helpers, such as the SpotLightHelper that can be used to show the angle of light.

Another way to see the light source is to create an object (such as a sphere) in the position of the light, which you can see here:

```
var lightDebug = new THREE.Mesh(new THREE.SphereGeometry(5), new THREE.MeshBasicMaterial());
lightDebug.position = light.position;
scene.add(lightDebug);
```

One way of using this version, which is what I prefer and I know many other people use the technique quite often, is to make the sphere quite small so that you can see it but it looks more like part of the animation rather than a debug mode.

Materials

You have seen a few materials used and mentioned, such as Phong, Lambert, and Basic–but what are they? Each type of material specifies the type of shading that is used. This is based on real-life materials and the differences between them, such as a plastic bottle appears different than a shiny can under the same lighting due to reflection, transparency, and so on. It is not possible to model the exact conditions we find in real life, but we can get quite close by modifying some properties and by using different shaders. At the time of writing, Three.js provides us with the built-in materials shown in Table 4-4.

Table 4-4. *Showing the built-in materials avaiable in Three.js.*

LineBasicMaterial	The LineBasicMaterial is used to create straight lines that by default are white and 1px wide.
LineDashedMaterial	This is similar to the LineBasicMaterial but is used to create dashed lines that are useful for debugging (though not limited to it), as you know it is not meant to be part of the scene.
MeshBasicMaterial	Depending on the wireframe property (defaults to false), this material is used to either draw flat or wireframe faces and is not affected by lighting. It is commonplace to use this for wireframes over the other materials since it has the least overhead. It is also commonly used for applying textures (images).
MeshDepthMaterial	This material is used to show depth and it is usually used in post processing.
MeshFaceMaterial	Quite often a shape will require different materials on each side, MeshFaceMaterial is effectively an array of materials.
MeshNormalMaterial	This is a useful material, especially for prototyping, since it makes sure each face is has a distinctive color and does not require lighting.
ParticleBasicMaterial	This is the material used by particle systems. The color defaults to white.
ShaderMaterial	If you would like to write your own shader (which will not be covered in this book), then this is the material you can use. It provides properties for GLSL such as fragmentShader, vertexShader, and uniforms.

There are two materials missing from Table 4-4, `MeshLambertMaterial` and `MeshPhongMaterial`. I will tackle these two separately from the list because they are somewhat similar and involve a lot of rendering techniques (too much for a list). We have already used Lambert as a generic 3D material but I didn't explain what it is. The simple explanation of the difference between the two materials, according to the current Three.js documentation is

- **Lambert**: A material for non-shiny (Lambertian) surfaces, evaluated per vertex.

- **Phong**: A material for shiny surfaces, evaluated per pixel.

This is generally enough for you to decide which to use for each situation, but I feel a more complete understanding is important and so I will briefly explain the technical differences and encourage you to look into them in more detail.

In computer graphics there are two models–which can both be combined –that determine the shading of the object; these are illumination and shading. Illumination uses ambient, diffuse, and specular to display light reflected (or refracted) off (or through) a surface. The math for shading is complicated, because it cannot be reduced to components, basically it shades (that is, works out the brightness) the faces using either flat shading or interpolated. The `MeshLambertMaterial` uses Gourand shading and Lambert illumination and by default the illumination is performed at each vertex and then interpolated across the face. `MeshPhongMaterial` uses both Phong shading and Phong illumination models and by default the vertex normals are interpolated across the surface and illumination is performed at each pixel (or more correctly, texel).

▓ **Note**   Three.js does not use perfect implementation of the algorithms, so if you are particularly interested in the mathematical models, then take that into consideration.

Data Visualizations

That's enough documentation for now, let's move on and make something useful. There are many types of data visualizations, from basic bar and pie charts to detailed globes and even models of solar systems. There are uses for all these, usually as a way to present the data to the public but also for data analysis. It is a vast subject area and so we will only be touching the surface of what you could visualize and how you could do it.

We could start anywhere, such as basic 3D graphics showing the government's financial data but that will quickly get boring so let's make a 3D node graph showing actors and actresses that have worked with each other (inspired by Six Degrees of Kevin Bacon). In this case, our nodes are the actors/actresses and the edges are films. I have provided some sample data as JSON to avoid the need to make you sign up to an API. This also means I can be more selective about the data because most of it is not needed.

3D Node Graph

Rather than jumping straight into using the data, it is best to instead just start with the graph. In this section all the nodes and edges will be random and it is entirely possible for two nodes to have multiple edges of the same edges. At this moment we needn't worry about that (it becomes much easier to handle once we have the real data).

We start with the basic setup that all scenes have, this time using both directional and ambient lights so that each node (which we will represent using random-colored spheres) has a nice effect.

```
var width  = window.innerWidth,
height = window.innerHeight;

var container = document.querySelector('#container');
```

```
var renderer = new THREE.WebGLRenderer();
renderer.setSize(width, height);
container.appendChild(renderer.domElement);

var VIEW_ANGLE = 45,
    NEAR = 0.1,
    FAR = 10000;
var camera = new THREE.PerspectiveCamera(45, width / height, 1, 1000);
camera.position.z = 600;

var ambient = new THREE.AmbientLight( 0x050505, 2 );
directionalLight = new THREE.DirectionalLight( 0xffffff, 1 );
directionalLight.position.set( 2, 1.2, 10 ).normalize();

var scene = new THREE.Scene();
scene.add(ambient);
scene.add(directionalLight);
scene.add(camera);

// The rest of the code for this section will go here.

function logic() {
  requestAnimationFrame(render);
}

function render() {
  renderer.render(scene, camera);
}

setInterval(logic, 1000/60);
```

You know how to make spheres and I am sure it would take you all of two seconds to work out how to position them randomly. However, what we need to do is randomly position spheres and we also need to randomly link them together with lines for edges. To do this, we have a Node object that stores the name and position and then generates the random edges. Because we are not currently using the data, the name defaults to "Random Node" and there is a getEdges() function that is accessed by the property edges that returns two random nodes to which to connect edges. To generate the random edges in getEdges we just need to multiply Math.random() by the amount of nodes, then round down (floor) because the indexes start from 0 not 1.

```
var amount_nodes = 20;

var Node = function() {
    name = "Random Node",
    position = new THREE.Vector3();

    function getEdges() {
        return [Math.floor(Math.random()*amount_nodes), Math.floor(Math.random()*amount_nodes) ];
    }
```

```
    return {
        name: name,
        edges: getEdges()
    }
}
```

To draw the graph we need three functions, one that draws a node and one that draws all of the edges of a node, we also need a function to draw the graph using the previous two functions. Let's start with drawNode(n), we take the node as a parameter so we have easy access to the node object we just made. Within the function we create a sphere using the same technique taught earlier, with a Lambert material of a random color. The random color is surprisingly easy to do, since hex (such as 0xffffff) is treated the same as any other number (it is after all just a representation of a number to a different base), we can do math on it, in this cause multiplying it by a random number. To find the position we choose a random number that is within the boundaries of an area that we specify, the area is then subtracted from this number to keep the graph in the center.

```
function drawNode(n)  {
    var radius = 10,
        segments = 50,
        rings = 50;

    var node = new THREE.Mesh(
        var material = new THREE.MeshLambertMaterial( {  color: Math.random() * 0xffffff } );
        var draw_object = new THREE.Mesh(
        new THREE.SphereGeometry(
            radius,
            segments,
            rings),
        material);
    );

    var area = 300;
    node.position.x = Math.floor(Math.random() * (area * 2 + 1) - area);
    node.position.y = Math.floor(Math.random() * (area * 2 + 1) - area);
    node.position.z = Math.floor(Math.random() * (area * 2 + 1) - area);

    n.position = node.position;
    scene.add(node);
}
```

Now we have the nodes drawn to the scene and it is time to connect them with the edges. Because these edges are random, as I said earlier, it is likely that some will double up causing thicker lines. This will not happen once we have added the data because we can use it to check whether a line has already been made. As you know from ambient lights, to have opacity you need to set transparent to true, so I have done this in LineBasicMaterial because the edges would be overwhelming if they were 100% white and opaque. To work out where the lines should go, we need to loop through the node.edges (which we randomly generate when a new node is created) and create a geometry that has a vertex at the current node's position and at the other node's (nodes[node.edges[i]]) position. Once that is created, we simply make a new line using the geometry and then add it to the scene.

```
function drawEdges(node)  {
    var line_material = new THREE.LineBasicMaterial( { color: 0xffffff, transparent: true, opacity:
0.1, linewidth:0.5 } );
    for (var i = 0; i < node.edges.length; i++)  {
```

```
        var tmp_geo = new THREE.Geometry();
        tmp_geo.vertices.push(node.position);
        tmp_geo.vertices.push(nodes[node.edges[i]].position);
        var line = new THREE.Line( tmp_geo, line_material );
        scene.add(line);
    }
}
```

Lastly, to finish this part of the project we just need to draw the graph using the two functions we just wrote. You may have noticed we were using an array called nodes, the nodes are created within drawGraph(). The first part of the function loops through the amount of nodes (amount_nodes) and creates a new Node object within the array, which it then draws using drawNode(). The edges have to be drawn afterward in a separate loop since drawEdges() uses the array of nodes to see which edges connect.

```
var nodes = [];
drawGraph();
function drawGraph()  {
    // Draw nodes
    for (var i = 0; i < amount_nodes; i++)  {
        nodes[i] = new Node();
        drawNode(nodes[i]);
    }

    // Draw edges, has to be done once we have the nodes in place
    for (var i = 0; i < amount_nodes; i++)  {
        drawEdges(nodes[i]);
    }
}
```

If you now put it all together, it should show a nice 3D node graph of random colors that does not represent anything (see Figure 4-3). This is a good starting point for a variety of visualizations and it should make you feel comfortable using the tools (namely Three.js) to produce more than just a simple shape.

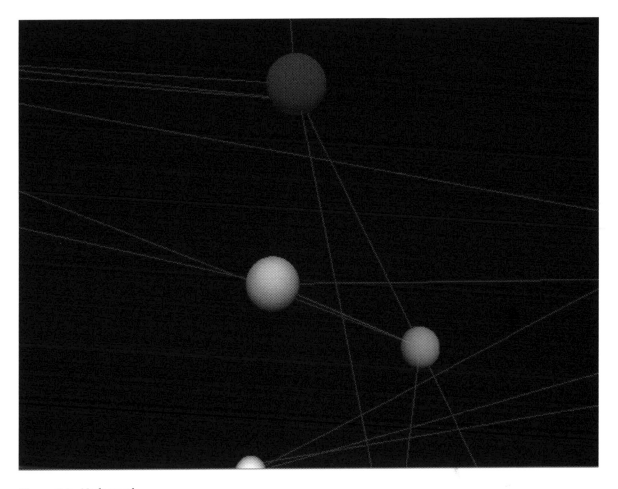

Figure 4-3. *Node graph*

I encourage you to fiddle with the code to make it your own. Here are a few ideas for how you can extend the graph:

- Use an API to visualize live data (Twitter, Government open data, etc.).

- Change size and/or color of the nodes based on the data.

- Add text overlays for hovering or clicking on the nodes and/or edges.

- Work on the navigation. It is hard to navigate a graph that has thousands of nodes. What works best–arrow keys? Mouse? Click to move? This is a good way to explore scale.

There are a lot of ways you could use the camera (some of which were explained earlier in the chapter) to navigate the graph. For now I have just been using the simple camera rotation technique, which is included in the code.

Adding Data

We have a node graph showing random nodes, it looks nice but there really isn't any meaning behind it. I have created a JavaScript file called data.js (with JSON in a variable called data to make it easy to access) that includes four actors/actresses and three movies. We will be using this to create a tiny node graph that shows the movies as edges between the nodes of the actors/actresses. Although there is not much data, this should give you a good idea of how the graph can be used for data visualization. Here is the data we will be using:

```
var data = {
    "People": [
        {
            "Id" : 0,
            "Name": "Tom Cruise",
            "Films": [1, 2]
        },
        {
            "Id" : 1,
            "Name": "Morgan Freeman",
            "Films": [1,3,5]
        },
        {
            "Id" : 2,
            "Name": "Bruce Willis",
            "Films": [3, 4]
        },
        {
            "Id" : 3,
            "Name": "Mary-Louise Parker",
            "Films": [3]
        }
    ],

    "Films": [
        {
            "Id": 0,
            "Name": "Oblivion",
            "Cast": [0, 1]
        },
        {
            "Id": 1,
            "Name": "Mission: Impossible",
            "Cast": [0]
        },
        {
            "Id": 2,
            "Name": "RED",
            "Cast": [1, 2, 3]
        },
```

```
        {
            "Id": 3,
            "Name": "Die Hard",
            "Cast": [2]
        },
        {
            "Id": 4,
            "Name": "The Shawshank Redemption",
            "Cast": [1]
        }
    ]
}
```

To create the graph we use the code we previously created but need to modify it to read the data object so that it links between the actors/actresses based on films they have been in. Although it is probably more useful to show every connection, I decided that for this example it would be best to only show when they are connected rather than having a separate line for each movie. I did this by checking whether the node was already in the array of edges of the other node.

The main change between this code and the previous is the drawGraph() function in which we now assign the people data to each node. Once the nodes are drawn, we need to go through each film and create edges in each node for every film by connecting each person to the person before them in the cast array, providing they have not already been connected.

```
drawGraph();
function drawGraph()  {
    var people = data["People"];
    var films = data["Films"];
    for (var i = 0; i < people.length; i++)  {
        nodes[i] = new Node();
        nodes[i].name = people[i].Name;
        nodes[i].films = people[i].Films;
        drawNode(nodes[i]);
    }

    for (var i = 0; i < films.length; i++)  {
        var cast = films[i]["Cast"];
        console.log(cast);
        if (cast.length > 1)  {
            for (var j = 1; j < cast.length; j++)  {
                if (nodes[cast[j-1]].edges.indexOf(cast[j]) == -1)  {
                    console.log(j)
                    console.log(nodes[cast[j-1]]);
                    nodes[cast[j-1]].edges.push(cast[j]);
                }
            }
        }
    }

    for (var i = 0; i < nodes.length; i++)  {
        drawEdges(nodes[i]);
    }
}
```

Finally, the name of the person that each node corresponds to should be shown. As we have already created a material for each node that gives a node its own color, we can use that to match the text color with the node. I've given the text a size and height (extrusion) of 10, but that is an arbitrary number that looked good–feel free to change it. Also, as I mentioned earlier, perhaps look into showing the text when a node has been clicked because as more nodes are added, the text will become harder to read. This should be added at the end of the drawNode function:

```
var text_object = new THREE.Mesh(new THREE.TextGeometry(node.name, { size : 10, height: 10}),
material);
    text_object.position.x = draw_object.position.x;
    text_object.position.y = draw_object.position.y;
    text_object.position.z = draw_object.position.z;
    scene.add(text_object);
```

Figure 4-4 shows the final outcome of this chapter, the node graph representing the data and showing the names alongside the nodes.

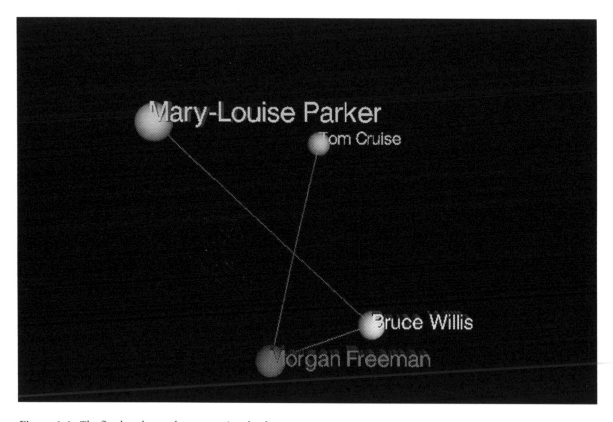

Figure 4-4. *The final node graph representing the data*

The entire code for this is available, as always, on either the Apress website at www.apress.com/9781430259442 or my own website at www.shanehudson.net/javascript-creativity.

Summary

In this chapter you have developed 3D skills from the basics of making an object appear to using it for data visualization. There is a wide variety of things you can do in just data visualization alone, let alone everything else you can do in a 3D world. Hopefully you now feel comfortable with Three.js. I encourage you to extend the examples in this chapter and to fiddle around with them, especially the node graph. In Chapter 5 we create music (or at least sound!) in the browser using the Web Audio API and SVG.

CHAPTER 5

■ ■ ■

Creating Music in the Browser

In Chapter 3 we used the Web Audio API to analyze audio by creating a simple visualization and a spectrogram. This chapter extends Chapter 3 by using the API to create music. To do this I introduce music theory and have a few examples before creating a web app that lets users create snippets of music using a basic synthesizer and to be able to move the snippets around the track to create their own music. This project is full of potential, so there are many routes you could take to modify it and make it your own, such as a full-fledged web-based Digital Audio Workstation.

Music Theory

This book is not about music theory, but in order to complete this project and to understand (or at least use) the Web Audio API it is quite important to understand the basics of music theory. Music is sound, and random sound is just noise, but since music is not noise, what makes music special? There are a number of aspects of music that are used to separate music from noise. These aspects include rhythm and tempo, but more importantly (from our point of view at least) it is the pitch and timbre that is at the heart of music, they are the aspects that create the instruments themselves. We do not need to be incredible musicians to create a tool that can be used for incredible music, we just need to focus on the aspects of the instrument itself and in this case our instrument is made using the Web Audio API and pitch is the frequency of the note.

So let's start right at the beginning, what is a note? Simply put, a note is a sound wave of a specific wavelength (the frequency that causes the pitch). Notes are named alphabetically in order of pitch from A to G (well...sort of), so a D is higher than a C. I said sort of because notes actually loop, in octaves, from C to C so A is higher than C of the same octave but lower than the C of the octave above it. Each frequency can be represented (both linguistically and practically) in hertz (hz). Due to the position on a piano, the C at frequency 261.63hz is called Middle C and is generally used as the note that calculations are relative to. For example, an easy to remember frequency is 440hz "A above Middle C."

Because every octave has the same notes at different frequencies and we already know a note is just a frequency itself, there must be a link between each octave because otherwise they fundamentally cannot be the same note. This link is ratio; each octave has the ratio of 2:1, so the wavelength of the note is double the octave before it. So to go from the A above Middle C to the A below Middle C we can simply do 440/2 = 220hz. This relationship is the fundamental concept behind harmony. Each note can be labeled with a number representing the octave, for obvious reasons, so for example Middle C is C3.

If you think of a piano, you will remember seeing the black keys spread in a pattern above the white keys; these keys are used to play the semitone (or half-step) between notes, which have a ratio of $2^{(1/12)}$. A semitone that is above a note will be its sharp, and the semitone below a note is its flat. So 466.16 is known as A# (A Sharp) or Bb (B Flat). These semitones are the most common example of "enharmonic equivalents" because they are technically two notes that are identical, the only difference being the direction of the music.

We don't have a piano, or a guitar, or any other instrument, so how do we plan to make music? When I explained what a note is, I called its frequency a *wavelength* because it is generated by sound waves. As you probably know, all sound waves are generated through vibrations. So all we need is the final piece of the puzzle, an oscillator; this is the basis of all sound synthesis, because it allows us to produce sound waves using just a speaker. *Sound envelope* is a term often used in sound synthesis 'that defines the sound of the wave, the term covers four components of sound: attack, decay, sustain, and release. By manipulating the sound envelope, you can begin to control the sound. Think of the differences between a piano and a triangle, they both have quite a high sustain (that is, they resonance for quite a while) but a triangle kind of "dings," whereas a piano sounds for a lot longer (depending of course on how long you play the note) so there is more attack for a piano than a triangle. In practice, it is hard to perfectly synthesis any instrument due to the amount of physics involved (such as the properties of a wooden piano) but by manipulating each note it gives you a way to attempt to replicate the sound of music through simply oscillating a waveform of your choosing.

Each sound wave has a shape (waveform) that visually represents the amplitude of the note over time, this has a lot of physics that we do not need to be concerned with but basically the amplitude is how the speaker needs to move to produce the sound. There are four basic waveforms, which make the basis of all sounds (see Figure 5-1).

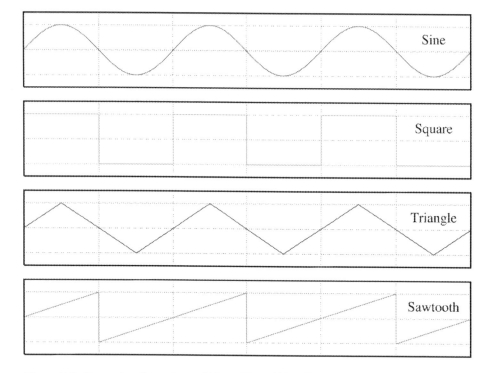

Figure 5-1. *Examples of waveforms.* `https://en.wikipedia.org/wiki/File:Waveforms.svg`

The four waveforms are

- **Sine wave:** This curved line follows the shape of the mathematical function sine.

- **Square wave:** A square wave is similar to binary, in that it is either at one frequency or the other.

- **Triangle wave:** The triangle wave is similar to the sine wave but is less smooth. This results in quite a sharp sound.

- **Sawtooth wave:** These waves are a combination of all the previous waves. This wave has the slow sharp sound of the triangle until it reaches the peak and then resets to the original frequency, much like the square wave.

Creating a Keyboard

Now that we've covered some basic theory, let's knuckle down and create a keyboard. There are many ways we could do this, such as using DOM or canvas but because keys are basic rectangles I have decided the best route is SVG as it is vector. To make it easy to create the SVG and to bind events to the keys (so that they can actually be used), we will be using a library called svg.js (this can be found at www.svgjs.com). A piano has 88 keys (52 white and 36 black), because this is a lot of keys to fit into an on-screen keyboard I have decided to include only the middle 3 octaves, giving us 21 white keys. Now, it does not make sense to allow the keyboard to only be used by a mouse because you cannot (unless on a multi-touch screen) press multiple keys without using the keyboard. Of course, a QWERTY keyboard only has nine letters on the middle row so I have decided to take S to K as playable white keys and use A or L to go down or up an octave. This is not a perfect solution because you may want to play more than one octave at a time, but for this project it is enough.

Let's start by defining an SVG using `var keyboard = SVG('keyboard');` this creates an SVG with an id of keyboard that can be accessed using a variable of the same name. With the SVG created we can now start adding the keys, the white keys are the easiest since we can just create keys with the width (and position) of the SVG divided by the amount of keys needed. Because these are the white keys, we need to set the attributes so that fill is white and stroke is black. Another attribute we need to set is the id so that we can modify the background (for key press) of the key later, this will be set to `"key"+i` so that we can easily access each key by iterating over the 21 keys.

```
var keys = [];
for (var i = 0; i < 21; i++) {
    keys[i] = keyboard.rect(width/21, height);
    keys[i].move(width/21 * i, 0);
    keys[i].attr({ fill: '#fff', stroke: '#000', id: "key"+i });
    // Event handlers go here
}
```

We need to add rectangles for the black keys also, but instead of being directly next to each other they are split into groups of 2 and 3, also the keys are just over half the height of the keyboard. To split the keys into groups, I have decided to keep it simple and just check to see whether i is one of the last keys of the group. If it is, then we add the width of a white key (`width/21`) to a variable called prevKey that we use to work out the position of the key.

```
var bkeys = [];
var prev = 0;
for (var i = 0; i < 15; i++) {
    bkeys[i] = keyboard.rect(width/42, height / 1.7);
    bkeys[i].attr({ fill: '#000', stroke: '#000', id: "bkey"+i });
    bkeys[i].move(prev + (width/(21*1.3)), 0);
    prev = prev + width/21;
    if (i == 1 || i == 4 || i == 6 || i == 9 || i == 11) {
        prev += width/21;
    }
    // Event handlers go here.
}
```

You now have a keyboard drawn to the screen, as seen in Figure 5-2.

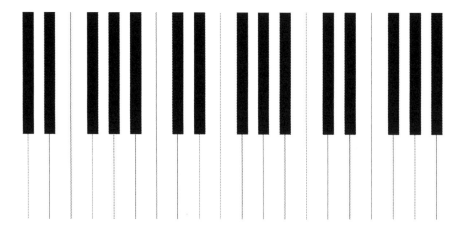

Figure 5-2. *The layout of the keyboard, consisting of three octaves*

Now that we have the keyboard layout created, we need to add the event handlers so that we can play sound as well as highlighting the key that has been pressed. Because we have two types of input (keyboard and mouse), quite a few event handlers are needed. SVG.js allows us to easily bind an event handler to each key, which makes it easy to handle the mouse by binding mousedown and mouseup to the keys. The keypress and keyup events are handled by adding event listeners to the window, which is the normal way of handling events. To bind the keys to the notes, we need to set up arrays for the top row of keys being black and middle row being white. We also need two arrays for each because keypress and keyup have different ids for each key. To get the correct note, because there are not enough keys on a computer keyboard for all the notes, we need to add the note position (using S to K as an octave) to the amount of keys in the octave multiplied by the current octave; this means that for black keys we use i + octave * 5 and for white we use i + octave * 7. For the mouse events we need to use closures to keep the counter because we need to bind the events for each key by binding within the for loops we just made, but if we do this without a closure then it will use i = 21 instead of the correct value. When a key has been pressed it needs to change color and then change back once the key has been released (this is true whether using mouse or keyboard). For the sound we will use functions called playSound(n) and stopSound(n), where n is the count that was originally i before the closure. These changes are shown in Listing 5-1.

Listing 5-1.

```
var keyboardKeys = [83,68,70,71,72,74,75];
var blackKeys = [69,82,89,85,73];

var keyboardPressKeys = [115,100,102,103,104,106,107];
var blackKeyPress = [101, 114, 121, 117, 105];

var octave = 1; // where octave 1 = middle C

var keys = [];
for (var i = 0; i < 21; i++) {
    keys[i] = keyboard.rect(width/21, height);
    keys[i].move(width/21 * i, 0);
    keys[i].attr({ fill: '#fff', stroke: '#000', id: "key"+i });
    keys[i].mousedown ((function(n) {
        return function() {
            var key = SVG.get("key"+n);
```

```
                key.fill({ color: '#f06' });
                playSound(n, false);
            }
        })(i));

        keys[i].mouseup((function(n)  {
            return function() {
                keys[n].fill({ color: '#fff' });
                stopSound(n, false);
            }
        })(i));
}

var bkeys = [];
var prev = 0;
for (var i = 0; i < 15; i++)  {
    bkeys[i] = keyboard.rect(width/42, height / 1.7);
    bkeys[i].attr({ fill: '#000', stroke: '#000', id: "bkey"+i });
    bkeys[i].move(prev + (width/(21*1.3)), 0);
    prev = prev + width/21;
    if (i == 1 || i == 4 || i == 6 || i == 9 || i == 11)  {
        prev += width/21;
    }

    bkeys[i].mousedown ((function(n) {
        return function()  {
            var key = SVG.get("bkey"+n);
            key.fill({ color: '#f06' });
            playSound(n, true);
        }
    })(i));

    bkeys[i].mouseup((function(n)  {
        return function() {
            bkeys[n].fill({ color: '#000' });
            stopSound(n, true);
        }
    })(i));
}

window.addEventListener('keypress', function(e) {
    for (var i = 0; i < keyboardPressKeys.length; i++)  {
        if (e.keyCode == keyboardPressKeys[i]) {
            var n = i + octave * 7;
            var key = SVG.get("key"+n);
            key.fill({ color: '#f06' });
            playSound(n, false);
        }
    }
    for (var i = 0; i < blackKeyPress.length; i++)  {
        if (e.keyCode == blackKeyPress[i]) {
```

```
                var n = i + (octave * 5);
                var key = SVG.get("bkey"+n);
                key.fill({ color: '#f06' });
                playSound(n, true);
            }
        }
    if (e.keyCode == 97 && octave > 0) --octave;
    if (e.keyCode == 108 && octave < 2) ++octave;
});

window.addEventListener('keyup', function(e) {
    console.log(e.keyCode);
    for (var i = 0; i < keyboardKeys.length; i++)  {
        if (e.keyCode == keyboardKeys[i]) {
            var key = SVG.get("key"+(i+octave*7));
            key.fill({ color: '#fff' });
            stopSound(i+octave*7, false);
        }
    }
    for (var i = 0; i < blackKeys.length; i++)  {
        if (e.keyCode == blackKeys[i]) {
            var n = i + octave * 5;
            var key = SVG.get("bkey"+n);
            key.fill({ color: '#000' });
            stopSound(n, true);
        }
    }
});
```

To play each note we need to have two arrays of oscillators, one for black and one for white. We connect each oscillator to a single gain node so that we have a node that we can use for recording the music, as well as potential for a volume changer. Obviously each oscillator needs to run at the correct frequency, we could automatically generate the frequencies but because we know exactly which keys will be used (and it is particularly awkward to generate them taking into consideration the gaps in the black keys) we can specify them in arrays like so:

```
var whiteNotes = [130.82, 146.83, 164.81, 174.61, 196, 220, 246.94, 261.63, 293.66, 329.63,
349.23, 392, 440, 493.88, 523.25, 587.33, 659.26, 698.46, 783.99, 880, 987.77];
var blackNotes = [138.59, 155.56, 185, 207.65, 233.08, 277.18, 311.13, 369.99, 415.3, 466.16,
554.37, 622.25, 739.99, 830.61, 932.33];
```

As you saw in the code for setting up the keys, the playSound and stopSound functions both take i and black as parameters so that we can know the position and the array that has the frequency for the note that is being played. Within playSound we select the oscillator and set both the frequency as well as the type and of course then turn it on using osc.noteOn(0).

- Sine wave = 0

- Square wave = 1

- Sawtooth wave = 2

- Triangle wave = 3

I have chosen sawtooth due to personal preference, but try them all and see what you think! The modified code is shown here:

```
function playSound(i, black) {
    stopSound(i, black);
    var freq;
    if (black) freq = blackNotes[i];
    else freq = whiteNotes[i];
    if (black) osc = ob[i];
    else osc = o[i];
    osc.type = 3;
    osc.frequency.value = freq;
    console.log(freq);
    osc.connect(gainNode);
    osc.noteOn(0);
    if (black) ob[i] = osc;
    else o[i] = osc;
}

function stopSound(i, black)  {
    if (black) osc = ob[i];
    else osc = o[i];
    if (typeof(o[i]) != "undefined") {
        osc.noteOff(0);
        osc.disconnect();
        osc = ctx.createOscillator();
    }
    if (black) ob[i] = osc;
    else o[i] = osc;
}
```

That's all you need to create a playable keyboard! The Web Audio API handles most of the low-level sound management, so you only need to connect the nodes and play the notes. I've used SVG.js but you could use anything else, create it from scratch, or even use a vector program such as Adobe Illustrator to export SVGs.

Recording the Music

Now that we have a working keyboard, we want to be able to record it and playback the output. Later in the chapter we will be adding functionality to move the music clippings around a track, so we need to store the music. So that we can use this as a standalone app, without requiring a server or complicating things for the user by asking them to download and upload the music , we will use local storage as a way to easily store and retrieve the music. Local storage works using key-value pairs, so we are going to need to name the music (which can be done either by user input or generating it based on the size of the local storage) and we also need to store the music as a value–this is the tricky bit.

I am not a fan of reinventing the wheel (and as I said, it is quite tricky), so to record the music to a wav encoded blob I have decided to use Matt Diamond's Recorder.js (this can be found at http://www.github.com/mattdiamond/Recorderjs). This library works by watching a specified Web Audio API channel, instead of connecting as normal, then enables a number of methods, including the method (exportWAV) that we will be using to get the audio as a blob.

■ **Note** To use Recorder.js you must be on a web server because it uses web workers to improve performance. One way to do this on your computer is to run `python -m SimpleHTTPServer`.

Let's start setting up the recorder by making it watch the gain node we created earlier. After that is done in the constructor, we then start recording.

```
var recorder = new Recorder(gainNode, { workerPath: "../recorderWorker.js"});
recorder.record();
```

As you can see, this makes it very easy to watch any audio that goes from `gainNode` to the output hardware. Now we need to create a function for recording the sound as well as playing it. When we call the `recordSound` method we need to store the blob (that is, the audio) as text (because `localStorage` does not allow objects to be directly stored) so we convert the object using `window.URL.createObjectURL`. To play the music we dynamically create a new Audio element (no need to append it to the DOM though) that has the src linking to the URL stored in `localStorage`. To make it scalable, so we can have a lot of music clippings, each function has a parameter called name that then becomes the key to the localStorage (where the object url is the value). Due to the way object URLs are created, to use them in any way you need to add them as the src of an audio element. Due to inefficiencies of doing so for every clip, it is instead best to work out the duration while it is recording and to add it alongside the object URL as an object that is then made into a string using JSON.

```
function recordSound(name)  {
    recorder.exportWAV(function(blob) {
        var object =  {
            file: window.URL.createObjectURL(blob),
            size: recordEnd - recordStart
        }
        localStorage[name] = JSON.stringify(object);
        drawTimeline();
    });
}

function playAudio(id)  {
    var audio = new Audio(JSON.parse(localStorage[localStorage.key(id)]).file);
    audio.play();
}
```

Using `Recorder.js` allows us to painlessly record anything that the Web Audio API can produce, be that generated notes or an input such as guitar. This makes it easy to store the recordings on the client side and play them back.

Timeline

Now that we have the keyboard working and have everything set up for recording the audio, let's create the interface. To avoid over complicating the project we will keep it simple and just have the keyboard with a timeline on which to put the music clippings, as well as buttons for recording and playing and stopping the timeline. When the page is loaded, the clips in the `localStorage` need to be represented as rectangles with a width proportional to the duration of the clip.

```
<!DOCTYPE html>
<html>
    <head>
        <title>Music Theory</title>
        <style>
            * { margin: 0; }
            body { background-color: #747e88; }
            a { color: #d4dfcf; cursor: pointer;}
            a:hover, a:focus  { color: #E4eee3; }

            .controls a { display: inline-block; padding: 10px; }
            .recording { background-color: #d68189; }
            #tracks  { height: 300px; width: 100%; }
            #keyboard  { height: 300px; position: relative; width: 100%; }
        </style>
    </head>
    <body>
        <div class="controls">
            <a id="record">Record</a>
            <a id="play">Play</a>
            <a id="stop">Stop</a>
        </div>

        <div id="tracks"></div>
        <div id="keyboard"></div>
        <script src="../svg.js"></script>
        <script src="../svg.draggable.js"></script>
        <script src="../recorder.js"></script>
        <script src="../recorderWorker.js"></script>
        <script src="script.js"></script>
    </body>
</html>
```

Starting with the buttons across the top of the page, each button needs an event listener for click events that have callbacks to do their specified task. The play and stop buttons just need to simply toggle a play variable that we will use to check whether the timeline bar for current time should be moving. The record button needs to toggle recording, this includes using the recorder to record the gain node, as well as toggling the recording class on the button and setting up the recordStart and recordEnd variables that are used to work out the duration. To get the name of the music clip we use a prompt. This could be done within the interface, but I used a prompt just for simplicity.

```
var toggleRecord = false;
var recordStart;
var recordEnd;
var recorder;
document.querySelector("#record").addEventListener('click', function() {
    if (!toggleRecord)  {
        recorder = new Recorder(gainNode, { workerPath: "../recorderWorker.js"});
        recorder.record();
        recordStart = Date.now();
        document.querySelector("#record").className = "recording";
        toggleRecord = !toggleRecord;
    }
```

```
    else {
        recordEnd = Date.now();
        document.querySelector("#record").className = "";
        toggleRecord = !toggleRecord;
        recordSound(prompt("Name of sound clipping:"));
    }
});

document.querySelector("#play").addEventListener('click', function() {
    play = true;
});

document.querySelector("#stop").addEventListener('click', function() {
    play = false;
});
```

With the buttons ready, let's start making the actual timeline. As with the keyboard, this uses SVG. An empty timeline simply has lines representing each track, so we need a variable for the amount of tracks (this makes it easy to change the amount needed) and to draw the lines we draw the amount of tracks + 1 so that it has a bottom border. The trackPos variable is used to know the height of each individual track, as well as to position each track in the correct place.

```
var timelineWidth = document.querySelector("#tracks").clientWidth;
var timelineHeight = document.querySelector("#tracks").clientHeight;
var tracks = SVG('tracks');

var play = false;

var numOfTracks = 5;
var track = [];
var trackPos = timelineHeight/numOfTracks;

var clippings = [];
drawTimeline();
function drawTimeline() {
    tracks.clear();

    for (var i = 0; i <= numOfTracks; i++) {
        track[i] = tracks.line(0, timelineHeight/numOfTracks, timelineWidth, trackPos);
        track[i].move(0, trackPos * i);
        track[i].attr({ stroke: '#DAC8B0', id: "track"+i });
    }
    // Clippings go here
}
```

The music clippings are rectangles on the same SVG as the timeline, because they are part of it, that represent the music based on the duration of the clip. Each rectangle needs to be draggable so that they can be moved around the tracks. We could use event listeners like we did in Chapter 2, but since we are using SVG.js we can just use the plugin for it that is found at https://github.com/wout/svg.draggable.js. To make the rectangles draggable we just need to include the script, then call .draggable() on the rectangle. Because the rectangle is within the timeline SVG, making it draggable means it can drag within that SVG not over the other components of the app. That said, it can still be dragged outside the SVG but cannot be seen, so we need to stop it from going out of the bounds. We also need to snap the rectangles between the tracks, to do this we need to check that the rectangle is within the boundary of each track and if it isn't, then to take the ceiling of the position so that it snaps to one of the tracks. Each rectangle also requires some text (that is moved with it) labeling the rectangle to the name of the music. In Figure 5-3 you can see how it looks when a few audio clippings have been recorded and placed in the timeline.

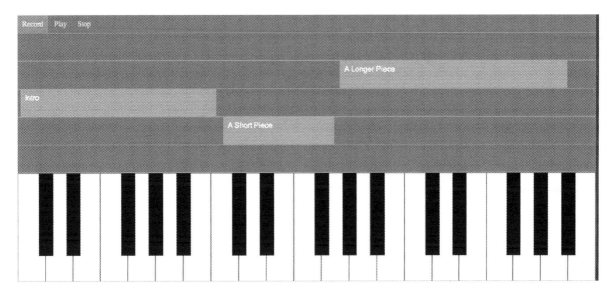

Figure 5-3. The finished project, showing the timeline with some pre-recorded music in separate tracks

In Listing 5-2, you can see the final modifications that are needed to make the rectangles draggable and snap on the timeline.

Listing 5-2.

```
var clippings = [];
drawTimeline();
function drawTimeline() {
    tracks.clear();

    for (var i = 0; i <= numOfTracks; i++) {
        track[i] = tracks.line(0, timelineHeight/numOfTracks, timelineWidth, trackPos);
        track[i].move(0, trackPos * i);
        track[i].attr({ stroke: '#DAC8B0', id: "track"+i });
    }
```

```
    for (var i = 0; i < localStorage.length; i++)  {
        var clipping = JSON.parse(localStorage[localStorage.key(i)]);
        clippings[i] = tracks.rect(timelineWidth/120 * clipping.size/120, trackPos);
        clippings[i].attr( { fill: "#C6A49A" } );
        clippings[i].move(150, trackPos * 3);

        var text = tracks.text(localStorage.key(i)).move(clippings[i].x() + 10, clippings[i].y() +
10).front();
        text.attr( { fill: "#fff", id: "text"+i });

        clippings[i].draggable();
        clippings[i].dragend = (function(text)  {
            return function() {
                if (this.y() < 0)
                    this.move(this.x(), 0);
                if (this.y() > timelineHeight - trackPos)
                    this.move(this.x(), height - trackPos);
                else
                    this.move(this.x(), Math.ceil(this.y() / trackPos) * trackPos);
                text.move(this.x() + 10, this.y() + 10);
            }
        })(text);

        clippings[i].dragmove = (function(text)  {
            return function() {
                text.move(this.x() + 10, this.y() + 10);
            }
        })(text);
    }
}
```

The finalized code for the chapter can be found in the usual place, the downloadable complement to the book on the Apress website at www.apress.com/9781430259442 or on my own website at www.shanehudson.net/javascript-creativity.

Summary

We now have the beginning of a music creation web app. From here there are many paths you can go down, such as changing the tone of the notes or adding the ability to mute tracks. We will be integrating this music creation app into the media player that we will be creating in the next chapter. Hopefully this has given you a good taste of what the Web Audio API can do, as well as some experience with SVG and local storage.

CHAPTER 6

■ ■ ■

The Music Player

So far, we have taken a brief tour through the winding roads of sound and graphics. We started with canvas and explored the world of 2D and animations; from there we crossed into looking at the video and audio html elements and web audio API from which we used canvas for visualizing music by creating tools such as spectrograms. It was then back into graphics to dive head first into 3D worlds where we played with types of lighting and materials to learn how things affect one another. Chapter 5 seemingly dropped the graphics altogether (except from using SVGs of course) and focused purely on music, generating notes through JavaScript without requiring any plugins or audio files, just a browser that implements the web audio API. I would, however, like to focus a little bit more on audio files by extending from Chapter 3 (where we looked at the codecs that are used and introduced the web audio API) and creating that media player I keep mentioning.

This chapter ties up all the loose ends of the previous chapters. We will make a media player that includes the music creation from the previous chapter as well as creating a 3D visualizer (based on Steven Wittens' js1k demo) that is less of a tool than the spectrogram and more like the art that you may remember seeing on media players such as Winamp.

Media Player

I would like to come at this from a different direction than the previous chapters. Earlier I taught you parts of a subject area, such as sound. Rather than teaching, I would like this chapter to feel more like a project to work on. There are so many ways to build a large app like this, as well as so many different features, that I'm going to define the specification of the app and it is your choice whether to tackle it the same way as I am or to take a different route.

Specification

Our music player must be client-side only, so there should be no reliance on servers except any that host music that is being played via a URL. There must be options from where to play the music, including the local machine and possibly services such as Tomahawk. Of course, as with any media player there must be pause, play, and stop buttons as well as functionality for at least one playlist. As I already mentioned, we will be integrating both the music creation app and a 3D visualizer into the media player. These will be integrated into the app but there is plenty of scope to take the app a lot further, such as developing a plugin system to separate out the functionality.

Where to Start

Now we need to think about the best way to organize the data and interface so that they are not too tightly linked but can affect each other. There are many ways to go about this, but because Backbone is very popular for doing exactly this, I am going to suggest we use Backbone. I am not going to presume any prior knowledge of it, although it isn't a tutorial about it either, so I will quickly explain each part of it as it is needed.

Playlists

The main function of a music player is to play the tracks within a playlist. So it makes sense to start with this functionality, where we can have a number of named playlists (the examples used are Latin and Reggae) that have tracks stored within them. The tracks should have a name, artist name, and URL. The URL can be used to play music from both local and remote sources, as well as the Data URIs that we used for storing the music in Chapter 5.

Models

In Backbone, there are both model and collection classes that can be created using `Backbone.Model.extend()` and `Backbone.Collection.extend()`, respectively. A *model* is simply an array that has been enhanced with Backbone features, and a *collection* is a way to store multiple models (this is a concept that is common in many programming languages but is not native within JavaScript). Each model can have defaults, which are simple objects used so that if part of the data is incomplete, then it will use the default. Collections have a property, called model, which defines the model class that should be used. I have decided to use a `localStorage` plugin for Backbone called `backbone.localstorage.js`, which can be added to the collection by adding the property `localStorage: new Backbone.LocalStorage("playlists")`.

To do this we need to separate the entities into models, so that the `Playlist` model has a name as well as an array of `Tracks` so that there can be a list of playlists that each have tracks and a name of their own. Each `Track` model has the name, artist, and URL as explained previously. The reason that we need a model for each playlist rather than just a collection of tracks is that collections cannot be named and of course the purpose of playlists is to separate tracks often into meaningful playlists such as the genre of music.

```
var Track = Backbone.Model.extend({
  defaults: {
      title: "Unknown",
      artist: "Unknown",
      url: "Unknown"
  }
});

var Playlist = Backbone.Model.extend({
  defaults: {
      title: "Untitled Playlist",
      tracks: []
  }
});

var Playlists = Backbone.Collection.extend({
  model: Playlist,
  localStorage: new Backbone.LocalStorage("playlists")
});

var playlists = new Playlists();
```

Views

We create views to display the models and collections using `Backbone.View.extend()`. A view is a way to encapsulate all the methods and event handlers of a model so that each looks after itself rather than worrying about lots of different data. It is also, perhaps more importantly, a way to connect to the data within the models to the templates that produce the HTML for rendering the data to the page. Usually one view would deal with a single model so that you would have to define just one model and one view. Unfortunately, views can handle collections but only as one collective model. We need to create list views that handle the model views, so that each model view can have an event attached to it rather than to the collection overall. So, to have an interface where there is both a list of playlist names as well as the playlist itself we need to have a list view for each as well as a view for each individual model. I have decided to call the list views PlaylistListView and TrackListView so that it is obvious they are list views. Of course I had to choose TrackList instead of Playlist so that the names were not duplicated and it is slightly more obvious what they mean. Each list has a view of the model it represents, PlaylistView and TrackView, of which there can be as many as needed per list view. Figure 6-1 shows a graphical representation of how these views are related.

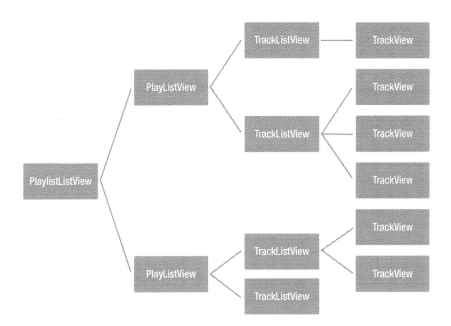

Figure 6-1. *A diagram showing the views required for an interface that has two lists with clickable list items*

The PlaylistListView is the view that lists each playlist by name, so it can be directly bound to a div with an id of playlists. This view is not responsible for any data that gets rendered to templates so we can go straight ahead and, inside the initialization, bind each model within the playlists collection to a function called renderItem that creates the playlistView for each playlist model in the collection and renders it to the screen. Of course, the view also requires a render function so that calls the renderItem on each model, I have done this by iterating through the models using Underscore's _.each to get the JSON of each model which it then passes to the renderItem function. The TrackListView works in the same way, rendering a TrackView for each Track model in the playlist's tracks array.

```
var PlaylistListView = Backbone.View.extend({

  el: "#playlists",
  model: playlists,

  initialize: function() {
      this.listenTo(this.model, "change", this.render);
      this.bind('render', this.render);
      _.bindAll(this, "renderItem");
  },
```

```
    renderItem: function(model){
        var playlistView = new PlaylistView({model: model});
        playlistView.render();
        $(this.el).append(playlistView.el);
    },

    render: function(){
      $("#playlists").html('');
      var self = this,
          html = '';
        _.each(this.model.toJSON(), function(mod) {
          self.renderItem(mod);
        });
    }

});

var TrackListView = Backbone.View.extend({
  el: $("#tracks"),

  initialize: function(){
      this.bind('changePlaylist', this.changePlaylist);
      _.bindAll(this, "renderItem");
  },

  renderItem: function(model){
      var trackView = new TrackView({model: model});
      trackView.render();
      $(this.el).append(trackView.el);
  },

  render: function(){
    $("#tracks").html('');
    if (this.model)  {
      var self = this,
          html = '';
        _.each(this.model.toJSON().tracks, function(mod) {
          self.renderItem(mod);
        });
    }
  },

  changePlaylist: function(current)  {
    if (!this.model && current) {
      this.model = current;
    }
    this.render();
  }

});
```

The individual views work in a similar way but of course they only have to render themselves and not the contents of the collection. These views also use underscore templates to render the data to the page. Each view has double-click events that trigger a function called play for the PlaylistView The play function triggers an event that causes App to play the first track on the playlist, whereas the play function on TrackView is used to play the specific track.

```javascript
var PlaylistView = Backbone.View.extend({

  tagName: "li",
  template: _.template($('#playlist-template').html()),

  events: {
    "dblclick"  : "play"
  },

  render: function() {
    var html = this.template(this.model);
    $(this.el).html(html);

    return this;
  },

  play: function()  {
    this.trigger('play');
  }
});

var TrackView = Backbone.View.extend({

  tagName: "li",

  template: _.template($('#track-template').html()),

  events: {
    "dblclick"  : "play"
  },

  render: function() {
    if(this.model)  {
      var html = this.template(this.model);
      $(this.el).html(html);
    }
    return this;
  },

  play: function()  {
    console.log("Playing " + this.model.title);
    player.trigger("play", this.model);
  }

});
```

Player Object

You will notice that I call a function on player, this is the object that is in control of managing the sound. By default the object stores el as a way to quickly access $("#player"), which is an audio element, it also stores the current track id as track and defaults to null. The state defaults to "paused" and is used to know whether a track is playing. To change the track we just need a setTrack function that sets track to be the new track id. Of course, the player needs to be able to play music so a play function is required; it needs to take a track id as an optional parameter so that it can be added to the src of the audio element.

```
var Player = Backbone.View.extend({
    el : "#player",

    track : null,

    state : "paused",

    initialize: function()  {
      this.bind('play', this.play);
      this.bind('pause', this.pause);
    },

    setTrack : function(track)  {
      this.track = track;
    },

    play : function(track)  {
      // If track is set then play new song. Else play current src (used for pausing).
      if (track)  {
        this.setTrack(track);
        $(this.el).attr("src", track.url).appendTo($(this.el).parent());
      }
      $("#togglePlaying").html("Pause");
      this.state = "playing";
      this.el.play();
    },

    pause : function()  {
      $("#togglePlaying").html("Play");
      this.state = "paused";
      this.el.pause();
    }
});
  var player = new Player();
```

Main App View

Okay, so we have lots of code to make up the basis of the app, but currently it will not actually do anything because none of the code is linked together. It is this view that is responsible for knowing the current playlist as well as managing all interactions between views (and any elements that are not in views). Due to the way that there is only ever one of each list view on the page, AppView handles the list views as singletons so that there can ever only be one of each in use.

So far all we need is a basic interface, consisting of elements for each view and two links that are used to trigger the prompts for new playlist and add tracks. These elements are just HTML elements that can be used in the same way as you would without Backbone, the only difference is that we also need to include the dependencies (including Backbone) as scripts.

```html
<div id="app">
    <a id="new-playlist">New Playlist</a>
    <a id="new-track">Add Track</a>
    <ul id="playlists"></ul>
    <ul id="tracks"></ul>
    <div id="player-controls">
      <a id="togglePlaying">Play</a>
    </div>
  </div>

  <audio id="player">

  <script src="../vendor/jquery.min.js"></script>
  <script src="../vendor/underscore.min.js"></script>
  <script src="../vendor/backbone.min.js"></script>
  <script src="../vendor/backbone.localStorage.js"></script>
  <script src="js/app.js"></script>
```

The data is handled using Underscore's templating engine. The templates are defined within script tags in the main HTML file.

```html
<script type="text/template" id="playlist-template">
    <li><%= title %></li>
  </script>

  <script type="text/template" id="track-template">
    <li>
      <%= title %>
      <%= artist %>
    </li>
  </script>
```

AppView is responsible for handling interactions with the DOM; the events are handled in Backbone by defining the type of event followed by a selector to find the elements and then a value that is the name of the function that should be triggered. The AppView will be using the models (such as playlists) that we created earlier in the chapter. You can see how the event listeners are set in the code that follows, as well as the structure that we will be using to develop the AppView.

```javascript
var AppView = Backbone.View.extend({
    el: $("#app"),

    currentPlaylist: -1, // Index of the playlist,
    trackListView : new TrackListView(),
    playlistListView : new PlaylistListView(),
```

```
  events: {
    "click #clear-completed": "clearCompleted",
    "click #toggle-all": "toggleAllComplete",
    "click #new-playlist":  "createPlaylist",
    "click #new-track":  "createTrack",
    "click #togglePlaying" : "togglePlay"
  },
  initialize: function() { },
  changePlaylist: function(id)  { },
  createPlaylist: function(e) { };
  createTrack: function(url) { },
  handleDrop: function(e) { },
  play: function()  { },
  preventDefault: function(e) { },
  render: function()  { },
  renderTracks: function() { },
  renderPlaylists: function() { },
  togglePlay: function()  { }
});
var App = new AppView;
```

Within the `initialize` function we will set up Backbone events (as opposed to DOM events) that trigger functions when events have been triggered on a model. The first function is `renderPlaylists`, the purpose of it is so that whenever the list of playlists needs changing, it can render on the `playlistListView` to update the playlists on the page. There is another function for rendering called `render`, which is used as a catchall to render both playlist and tracks. The render function calls both `renderPlaylists` and `renderTracks`. The latter works by making sure the playlist to be rendered (the actual tracks within the playlist, that is) has the current id held within `currentPlaylist`. However, it should always be correct already because to change playlist in the first place we have a `changePlaylist` function that both changes the `currentPlaylist` id as well as changing the playlist model for the `trackListView`.

```
changePlaylist: function(id)  {
  this.currentPlaylist = id;
  this.render();
},
render: function()  {
  this.renderTracks();
  this.renderPlaylists();
},
renderTracks: function() {
  if (this.currentPlaylist != -1)  {
    var current = playlists.get(this.currentPlaylist);
    this.trackListView.trigger('changePlaylist', current);
  }
},
renderPlaylists: function() {
  this.playlistListView.trigger('render');
}
```

We are now left with two more functions to create—the functions for adding new playlists and tracks. It is very simple to create a new playlist, because we can get the playlist name through a prompt and then just create a new playlist using Backbones' `create` function on the `playlists` collection. For the `createTrack` function, however, we have quite a lot more work to do. We need to get the `trackName`, `trackArtist`, and `trackUrl`, all of which we can ask for using prompts, except for when a URL is passed to the function (such as for the drag and drop functionality that we will add shortly) in which case that URL is used as trackUrl. We then need to check whether there is a playlist with tracks in it. If a currentPlaylist has not been set, then we just use the first playlist if any exists. Because the tracks are stored within an array inside a model, we have to work around the default Backbone behavior a bit as you can replace the array but not add to it. To do so we retrieve the current array of tracks and then add the new track to that array. With the new track in the array we can overwrite the array in the model with the "new" array that includes the track. With that done, it is now time to render the tracks to the page.

```
createPlaylist: function(e) {
  var playlistName = prompt("Playlist Name");
  playlists.create({title: playlistName});
},

createPlaylist: function(e) {
  var playlistName = prompt("Playlist Name");
  playlists.create({title: playlistName});
},

createTrack: function(url) {
  var trackName = prompt("Track name");
  var trackArtist = prompt("Track artist");
  var trackUrl = (typeof(url) === "string") ? url : prompt("Track url");
  if (trackName && playlists.models[0]) {
    if (this.currentPlaylist===-1) this.currentPlaylist = playlists.models[0].id;
    var tracks = playlists.get(this.currentPlaylist).get("tracks");
    tracks.push({ title: trackName, artist: trackArtist, url: trackUrl });
    playlists.get(this.currentPlaylist).save({ tracks : tracks});
    this.renderTracks();
  }
},
```

Drag and Drop

If you stretch your memory back to Chapter 2, you will remember that we used drag and drop functionality for the coloring book app. Dragging files is quite an obvious way to get a file into the app, so it makes sense to use it as a way to add new tracks. This version adds the dropped track to the current playlist but I recommend you modify it to try to add tracks to a playlist by dropping it on the playlist's name. I have reworked the original code we had in Chapter 2 so that you can see how similar it is to use drag and drop functionality on other types of files. We start by setting up the event listeners to call preventDefaults and handleDrop as needed. The handleDrop function is used to select the first file out of the dropped files and forward it to createTrack, which is the function in the main App view that adds the track to the playlist. This is a good example of leveraging code that has already been written to easily add new functionality! Unfortunately we cannot directly use Backbone events because there is (at the time of writing) no way to stop the event bubbling. To get the track name and artist I have decided that prompts are the easiest way to do it. There are two more opportunities for improving the code here, which I encourage you to try, these are to enable multiple file drops and to improve the interface so that prompts are not required (or you could perhaps try to get the data from the metadata of the file).

In the AppView initialize function, we put the event listeners:

```
window.addEventListener('dragover', this.preventDefault, false);
window.addEventListener('dragenter', this.preventDefault, false);
window.addEventListener('drop', this.handleDrop, false);
```

We also need the `handleDrop` and `preventDefault` functions in the `AppView`:

```
handleDrop: function(e) {
    e.stopPropagation();
    e.preventDefault();
    var file = e.dataTransfer.files[0];

    reader = new FileReader();
    reader.readAsDataURL(file);
    reader.onload = (function(theFile) {
      return function(e) {
        App.createTrack(e.target.result);
      };
    })(file);
},
preventDefault: function(e) {
  if (e.preventDefault) {
    e.preventDefault();
  }
  return false;
},
```

Integrating the Music Creation

Let's now integrate the music creation from the previous chapter so that we can create our own tracks to add to the playlists. It sounds like a simple task, and it mostly is, but we made the creator work in such a way that the `localStorage` with playlists in it will muck it up (because it uses a counter as an id instead of a hash). So we need to fix that first!

Currently the key of each `localStorage` record of the music creation app is used within a counter to iterate over and to find any particular clipping. This is generally quite a bad approach because if an id is removed, then it could break the loop and also, as I just mentioned, it does not play well when there are other types of key-value pairs in the storage. If you take a look at the `localStorage` that was produced using the Backbone plugin, you will see that the keys all have a string prepended as a kind of namespace for the key. There is also a single key of the same name as the namespace, the value of which is a list (read: `JSON.stringifiy`'ed array) containing each clipping name so that we can still iterate over all the keys by taking each name in the array and finding the corresponding key.

Within the `recordSound` function, we need to change it so that the object is now stored correctly with the namespace before the key. It also needs to add the key to the value of the namespace, as explained, so we need to check whether it exists so that we can either add to it or make a new one. Whenever data needs to be accessed, you can use `JSON.parse(localStorage["clippings-" + clippingNames[i]])`.

```
function recordSound(name)  {
  recorder.exportWAV(function(blob) {
      var object = {
          file: window.URL.createObjectURL(blob),
          size: recordEnd - recordStart
      }
      if (localStorage["clippings"]) {
          var clippings = JSON.parse(localStorage["clippings"]);
          clippings.push(name);
          localStorage["clippings"] = JSON.stringify(clippings);
      }
```

```
    else {
        localStorage["clippings"] = JSON.stringify([name]);
    }
    localStorage["clippings-"+name] = JSON.stringify(object);
    drawTimeline();
    });
}
```

The final version of the keyboard with the changes made can be found in the online download available from the Apress website at www.apress.com/9781430259442 or my own website at www.shanehudson.net/javascript-creativity.

Music Visualization

Most of what we have gone through so far has rules, such as design patterns or music theory. This step does not. You can think of music visualization as an art, most of the mathematics we use are loosely based on concepts such as trigonometry from which we can fiddle the numbers to make the visualization look interesting. I have been very inspired by Steven Wittens (http://www.acko.net) who has been active in this space by writing articles, speaking at conferences, and creating demos that all use math to create interesting effects. For this section I have modified Steven's js1k entry to use with the music player, because he has already written an in-depth article (http://acko.net/blog/js1k-demo-the-making-of) about it which I highly recommend reading!

The visualization, shown in Figure 6-2, is a 2D canvas with curved lines on which squares move along to the tempo of the music. Because it is based on Steven's article, I will not go into too much detail but I would like to pick out some of the key aspects that can often be used in other projects so first take a look at the full code listing for visualizer.js. I have tried to clean the code up but because it was originally created to be very well optimized, there are still some parts that may not use best practices.

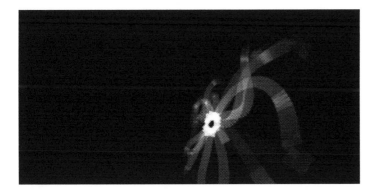

Figure 6-2. *Music visualization while playing Bassa Island Game Loop by Kevin MacLeod*

```
// Polyfill for RequestAnimationFrame
(function() {
  var requestAnimationFrame = window.requestAnimationFrame || window.mozRequestAnimationFrame ||
                        window.webkitRequestAnimationFrame || window.msRequestAnimationFrame;
  window.requestAnimationFrame = requestAnimationFrame;
})();
```

```
function visualizer() {
    w = $('#visualizer').width();
    h = $('#visualizer').height();
    g = $('#visualizer')[0].getContext("2d");
    ratio = w / h;
    g.globalCompositeOperation = "lighter";
    g.scale(w / 2 / ratio, h / 2);
    g.translate(ratio, 1);
    lw = 45 / h;
    a = r = d = 0;
    Xt = Yt = Zt = Xi = Yi = Zi = x = y = z = X = Y = Z = frames = 0;
    lastPointVisible = false;
    time = u = -8;
    requestAnimationFrame(draw);
}

function draw() {
    freqData = new Uint8Array(analyser.frequencyBinCount);
    analyser.getByteFrequencyData(freqData);
    if (!$("#player")[0].paused)  {
        var average = getAverage(freqData);
        console.log(average);
        //console.log(freqData);
        if (average > 0)  {
            for (frames = 0; frames < 70; frames++) {
                Xt = (average/100) * 18 - 9;
                Yt = (average/100) * 18 - 9;
                Zt = (average/100) * 18 - 9;
            }

            Xi = interpolate(Xi, Xt);
            Yi = interpolate(Yi, Yt);
            Zi = interpolate(Zi, Zt);

            X  = interpolate(X,  Xi);
            Y  = interpolate(Y,  Yi);
            Z  = interpolate(Z,  Zi);

            yaw   = Math.atan2(Z, -X * 2);
            pitch = Math.atan2(Y * 2, Math.sqrt(X * X + Z * Z));

            time += 0.05;
            g.clearRect(-ratio, -1, 2 * ratio, 2);
            for (i = 16; i; --i) {
                v = 0;
                for (pointIndex = 45; pointIndex;) {
                    pointIndex--;
                    offset = time - pointIndex * 0.03 - i * 3;
                    longitude = Math.cos(offset + Math.sin(offset * 0.31)) * 2
                            + Math.sin(offset * 0.83) * 3 + offset * 0.02;
                    latitude = Math.sin(offset * 0.7) - Math.cos(3 + offset * 0.23) * 3;
```

```
                distance = Math.sqrt(pointIndex+.2);
                z = Math.cos(longitude) * Math.cos(latitude) * distance;
                y = Math.sin(longitude) * Math.cos(latitude) * distance;
                z = Math.sin(latitude) * distance;

                x -= X; y -= Y; z -= Z;

                x2 = x * Math.cos(yaw) + z * Math.sin(yaw);
                y2 = y;
                z2 = z * Math.cos(yaw) - x * Math.sin(yaw);

                x3 = x2;
                y3 = y2 * Math.cos(pitch) + z2 * Math.sin(pitch);
                z3 = z2 * Math.cos(pitch) - y2 * Math.sin(pitch);
                h = !pointIndex;
                g.lineWidth = lw * (2 + h) / z3;
                x = x3 / z3;
                y = y3 / z3;
                g.lineTo(x,y);
                distance = Math.round(45 - pointIndex) * (1 + h + Math.max(0, Math.sin(time *
6 - pointIndex / 8) - .95) * 70);
                g.strokeStyle = "rgb(" + Math.round(distance * (Math.sin(h + i + time * .15)
+ 1)) + "," + Math.round(distance * (h + Math.sin(i - 1) + 1)) + "," + Math.round(distance * (h +
Math.sin(i - 1.3) + 1)) + ")";
                if (z3 > 0.1) {
                  if (lastPointVisible) {
                    g.stroke();
                  }
                  else {
                    lastPointVisible = true;
                  }
                }
                else {
                  lastPointVisible = false;
                }
                g.beginPath();
                g.moveTo(x,y);
              }
            }
          }
        }
    requestAnimationFrame(draw);
}

function getAverage(freqData)  {
    var average = 0;
    for (var i = 0; i < freqData.length; i++)  {
        average += freqData[i];
    }
    average = average / freqData.length;
    return average;
}
```

```
function interpolate(a,b) {
    return a + (b-a) * 0.04;
}
```

The beginning is just setup code like we usually use for canvas, grabbing the context and the dimensions. After these lines however is a very powerful line of code, `g.globalCompositeOperation = "lighter"`. If you have experience with computer graphics on a technical level or have used blending modes in Photoshop (or another graphics package), then you will have an idea of what this does. Composite operations are a form of compositing (alongside clipping) that are used for manipulating (based on a number of commonplace algorithms) multiple shapes depending on how they overlap. The composite operators themselves are known as Porter-Duff operators (after their inventors) but have slightly different names when used with canvas. There are many composite operations. Here we are using `lighter`, which just makes any overlapped area of shapes so that the color is a lighter blend of the overlapped shapes. The default is `source-over`. Table 6-1 is a full list of available operations (from the canvas spec):

Table 6-1.

Operation Name	Porter-Duff Operator	Description
source-atop	A atop B	Display the source image wherever both images are opaque. Display the destination image wherever the destination image is opaque but the source image is transparent. Display transparency elsewhere.
source-in	A in B	Display the source image wherever both the source image and destination image are opaque. Display transparency elsewhere.
source-out	A out B	Display the source image wherever the source image is opaque and the destination image is transparent. Display transparency elsewhere.
source-over	A over B	Display the source image wherever the source image is opaque. Display the destination image elsewhere. This is the default operation.
destination-atop	B atop A	Same as `source-atop` but using the destination image instead of the source image and vice versa.
destination-in	B in A	Same as `source-in` but using the destination image instead of the source image and vice versa.
destination-out	B out A	Same as `source-out` but using the destination image instead of the source image and vice versa.
destination-over	B over A	Same as `source-over` but using the destination image instead of the source image and vice versa.
lighter	A plus B	Display the sum of the source image and destination image, with color values approaching 255 (100%) as a limit.
copy	A (B is ignored)	Display the source image instead of the destination image.
xor	A xor B	Exclusive OR of the source image and destination image.

The next portion of the code uses a ratio to scale and translate the canvas. Strictly speaking, this isn't needed. But I have decided to keep it because it is an interesting approach to optimization. Basically instead of plotting the coordinates of the entire canvas, we will be plotting them between −1 and 1, so that the performance is improved, as transforming the canvas is easier and quicker than individually plotting the entire thing. The `lastPointVisible` boolean is another slight optimization that is used to only render the foreground so that nothing in the background that cannot be seen is rendered anyway. From here we need to use `requestAnimationFrame` for the same reasons as before, to keep it smooth and to only process (this is of course very intensive code) when needed. The `RAF` calls a `draw` function that draws each frame. As an aside, are you seeing the patterns yet? Every project can be reduced to just a few patterns, which is why I use examples that you will probably never need to build—the concepts will be useful regardless!

Within the `draw` function we grab the frequency data. Now we have a bit of a dilemma... how to use the data? For this example I have decided to just use the average frequency to move the lines in the visualization, but there are many options for playing around with this. One good idea might be to work out the beats per minute or to have separate lines representing ranges of frequencies.

The full code listing is, as always, available on both the Apress website at `www.apress.com/9781430259442` and on my own website at `www.shanehudson.net/javascript-creativity`.

Summary

That was a particularly long project so I made sure to only explain the concepts or code that were not already pretty obvious; hopefully you did not get lost along the way. Of course, a music player has such wide scope that this chapter barely scrapes the edges of what you can do so I chose the features that would teach you the most skills for using in other projects. I strongly encourage you to explore other avenues of the project, such as adding a plugin system or converting the music visualizer into 3D (currently it gives the effect of 3D but is only shown in 2D). I glossed over a lot of the math for the visualization because I am trying to explore creative things we can make with JavaScript rather than teaching math, but I strongly recommend reading Steven Wittens' article on the making of his js1k demo at `http://acko.net/blog/js1k-demo-the-making-of`.

CHAPTER 7

Real-time Collaboration with Node.js

Throughout the book so far, all the code we have written has been client side, but although client side JavaScript is very powerful nowadays it is often necessary to have a server so that data can be stored online, to keep sensitive logic out of the client, or so that users can interact with each other online. You may be familiar with other server side languages such as PHP or Ruby (possibly even Perl!), but one of the advantages of Node.js is that you write server side code in JavaScript so it should be easy to pick up because you have client side JS experience.

Making a Chatroom

In this chapter we use Node.js with Socket.IO to create a real time chatroom web app that allows multiple users to talk to each other. I guide you through setting up Node.js on your local machine because most commonly used servers (shared hosting) do not support Node.js, but do be aware that some services such as Heroku and Amazon Web Services do have free tiers.

Installing Node.js

Obviously to write anything using Node.js, you need to have it installed. There are many ways to install it. You can use a package manager such as apt-get, yum, or Homebrew (depending on which operating system you are using) but these are not always up to date. On the Node.js website, www.nodejs.org, you can download the latest version executable binaries or build it from source code. Alternatively, you can use the Node Version Manager (nvm) from www.github.com/creationix/nvm, which is particularly useful if you are working with many codebases that are not all using the latest version. Node comes with a built-in package manager called npm, which handles dependencies using a file called package.json, so rather than installing Express and Socket.IO yourself, you just put it in the file. When you are ready to install the packages, run npm install within the folder that has package.json.

```
{
  "name": "javascript-creativity-chatroom",
  "description": "A chatroom made in chapter 7 of the JavaScript Creativity book.",
  "version": "0.0.1",
  "private": true,
  "dependencies": {
    "express": "3.x",
    "socket.io" : "0.9.x"
  }
}
```

Unlike traditional JavaScript, Node.js has a module system that allows you to load JavaScript files at runtime. Each module is defined in a file, exporting variables and functions through a `module.exports` object. In another file, you can use the `'require'` function to load the module and get to its `module.exports` contents. There are three different ways to load a module.

- `require()` a relative file, for example `require('./lib/utils.js')`. This requires the single file and returns the value of `'module.exports'` in that file. You'll use this method quite a lot if you have large, multi-file projects.

- `require()` a core module, which are special keywords, for example `require('http') to load the core http module`. Node.js comes installed with a host of standard core modules, but they are not included by default, meaning you have to require them when you want them. You can see the full list of core modules in the Node.js documentation (`www.nodejs.org/api/index.html`).

- `require()` a distinct module from a `node_modules` folder, for example `require('express')`. This is the most powerful feature of the module system. You can require entire separate modules by referencing the module name. The way this works is that Node.js has special knowledge of the node_modules folder. It walks up the directory tree from the current script, looking for `node_modules/<name>/package.json` or `node_modules/<name>/index.js`. It looks at the package.json first, is to see whether it has a "main" property, which references a .js file to load that is named differently to index.js. Let's say you have a file /www/myapp/`index.js`, in this file you have `require('express')`. Node.js looks for the module in the following directories:

  - `/www/myapp/node_modules/express/`(package.json or index.js)

  - `/www/node_modules/express/`(package.json or index.js)

  - `/node_modules/express/`(package.json or index.js)

  - `$NODE_PATH/express/`(package.json or index.js)

  - `$HOME/.node_modules/express/`(package.json or index.js)

  - `$HOME/.node_libraries/express/`(package.json or index.js)

  - `$PREFIX/lib/node/express/`(package.json or index.js)

  - This is an exhaustive list of the folders Node.js looks in; it is highly recommended that you ensure your modules are placed in the local node_modules folder, for speed and reliability. The other folders are mostly useful for when Node.js modules inside a node_modules folder require their own modules, so you can share modules between your project and your modules.

This is where npm steps in to make things even better. Due to the features of node_modules folders in Node.js, npm looks at the "dependencies" and "devDependencies" objects in your package.json, and download each to your node_modules folder. It also downloads all your modules' dependencies, and your modules' modules' dependencies, and so on. The difference between "dependencies" and "devDependencies" is that npm will not install devDependencies of other modules, only dependencies. By default npm installs everything into the local node_modules folder. This isn't always what you want, so if you install modules with `npm install -g <module>`, then it installs them globally (typically in `$HOME/.node_modules/`). This is really useful as you can use this to install command line programs written in Node.js. For example I use nodemon by Remy Sharp as an alternative way to run the node server while I am developing a project, because the default `node [filename]` approach to running a server does not watch for files that have been updated while the server is running. To install nodemon you run `npm -g install nodemon`, then run `nodemon [filename]` to run a server through nodemon. More information about nodemon can be found at `www.remy.github.io/nodemon/`.

The simplest example of Node.js is, of course, Hello World. To serve a web page we need to require a module called http, which lets us handle the low-level aspects of HTTP. This module is a core module, so we use the first definition in the list. Once HTTP is required, we store it within a variable called http. We then use a method on http called createServer; this has a callback that lets you send a response (also known as the web page). To create the web page that gets served, we start by writing the headers using response.writeHead. The first parameter that needs to be provided is the HTTP status code 200 (OK). The second is the actual header, in this example we are only writing "Hello World" so the Content-Type can be text/plain, you may choose to use text/html if you want to write some HTML to the page. To write the actual content, you just use response.write. Once you've finished writing the response, end it with response.end(). Now you have a server but to actually serve the page you need to tell it to listen for activity on a port (in this case, port 8080).

```
var http = require("http");
http.createServer(function(request, response) {
  response.writeHead(200, {"Content-Type": "text/plain"});
  response.write("Hello World");
  response.end();
}).listen(8080);
```

Now that you know how to require a module and do something with it, let's make our own simple module that makes use of the module.exports that I mentioned. This module will wrap up our Hello World code into a file called helloworld.js, which we then require as a variable called hello in server.js and call the server method.

helloworld.js

```
var http = require("http");

function hello() {
  http.createServer(function(request, response) {
    response.writeHead(200, {"Content-Type": "text/html"});
    response.write("Hello World");
    response.end();
  }).listen(8080);
}

module.exports.server = hello;
```

server.js

```
var hello = require('./helloworld.js');
hello.server();
```

Of course, this is an incredibly simplistic example but it shows you quite nicely how you can require a custom module and call a method based on the name that it is exported as rather than the name of the function. It may help to point out here the differences between a method and a function, because many people use them interchangeably (which is fine, but I prefer to be more specific). A method is used on an object, while a function is independent of any object.

Socket.IO and Express

I mentioned Socket.IO earlier, it was one of the packages we installed from package.json, but I did not explain what it does. Basically it is a wrapper for web sockets so that all browsers can support real-time communication.

Socket.IO aims to make real-time apps possible in every browser and mobile device, blurring the differences between the different transport mechanisms. It's care-free real-time 100% in JavaScript.

Socket.IO homepage

Socket.IO is also incredibly easy to use. Once it is installed, it needs to be required within the server-side files (similar to requiring a file in PHP, but node automatically finds the location that it is installed) and then set it to listen to the server.

Of course, we have not yet made a server. Languages such as PHP execute once per file and translate the file's contents into an output, Node.js is different in that it is a long-standing process that will serve many files many times. Node.js includes an HTTP module, although you can use apache or nginx if you want, that gives you the capability of creating a simple server yourself—but for most situations you don't want to be mucking around with low-level server code.

Express.js makes it easy to get to the actual code-writing part of developing a website, rather than worrying about how each file can access the rest of the file structure and so on. However, it isn't very opinionated; with Express.js you can use any paradigm (or way of working) that you like. You can write simple websites, blogs, advanced web apps, or a REST API using the tools that Express provides. If you do prefer an opinionated approach, there is an official structuring tool for Express called express-generator that can be installed globally using npm to help you get started on a new project, although it doesn't force you to keep using the same structure.

As a brief example of using Express to manage the low-level code, see the two code snippets that follow. They both write 'Hello World!' to the page if you are on localhost:8080/hello, and they write 'Goodbye cruel world!' if you are on any other page. The difference is that the first snippet directly uses the http and the second snippet uses Express. Of course this barely scratches the skin of what Express is capable of, but it should show you nicely how Express does not require the lower-level code such as HTTP headers.

Without Express

```
var http = require('http');
http.createServer(function(request, response) {
  var url = request.url;
  response.writeHead(200, {"Content-Type": "text/html"});
  if (url == '/hello')  {
    response.write("Hello World!");
  }
  else  {
    response.write("Goodbye cruel world!");
  }
  response.end();
}).listen(8080);
```

With Express

```
var express = require('express');
var app = express();
app.get('/hello', function(request, response) {
  response.send("Hello World!");
});
app.get('/*', function(request, response) {
  response.send("Goodbye cruel world!");
});
app.listen(8080);
```

Now let's use Express to begin the writing the server for our chatroom. At the beginning of the chapter there was a package.json for installing Express and Socket.IO, if you haven't yet installed those packages, then you will need to do so now. Using Socket.IO is slightly different than using Express on its own in that it requires an http.createServer instance to be passed to Socket.IO's listener. This was changed in version 3 of Express, prior to that the express() function returned an instance of http.Server.

```
var app = require('express')(),
    server = require('http').createServer(app),
    io = require('socket.io').listen(server);
server.listen(8080);
```

Currently there is nothing to see, because we didn't even write 'Hello World' to the page this time, so let's set up a basic page using just HTML. For the most basic chatroom, all we need is two text boxes to put your name and message in (you could do name differently depending on UI choices) as well as a button to send the message and a div (you could use a list to improve semantics) to put the messages in. This file can be (although doesn't have to be) saved as index.html in the same folder as the server code, as you would normally.

```
<!doctype html>
<html>
    <head>
        <title>Chatroom</title>
    </head>
    <body>
        <label for="nickname">Nickname:</label><input type="text" id="nickname"></input>
        <div id="messages"></div>
        <textarea id="message"></textarea>
        <a id="send">Send</a>
    </body>
</html>
```

Now you need to use routers (as we did in the Hello World example) to tell the browser where to find content. For this chatroom, we want multiple rooms to be accessible and a nice way to do this is have the name of the chatroom (or a random identifier) in the URL of the room. Express has a way to easily check for this name, as a pathname segment (also known as a named parameter), but because this chatroom does not need multiple views, we can just direct every page to index.html. We could use a wildcard for this instead of a pathname segment, but it is a nice way to introduce the idea of pathnames being used as parameters. It is also a way to force a chatroom id to be included, as it will not serve the page without any id; this means that a separate route would be needed if you want to add a homepage.

```
app.get('/:id?', function (req, res) {
    res.sendfile(__dirname + '/index.html');
});
```

Of course, this is a rather useless chatroom. Let's write the server-side code for dealing with messages. Using Socket.IO we need to check for a connection, using io.sockets.on('connection', function (socket) {}); as an event handler for any connections, then join the room that is named in the pathname segment. Unlike Express, to get the identifier we use var room = socket.handshake.headers.referer as the Express .get call is not available once it has already been routed. Other ways to get the identifier would be to send the pathname segment from the client side or to initially serve it using a res.local (variables scoped to the request/response cycle) and exposing as a global variable on the client side. Using socket.handshake is quite long but in this case it is a nice way to avoid sending from the client side.

With the identifier stored in a variable called room, we can now use socket.join(room); to join a Socket.IO room with the same name as the ID. These rooms are basically a way to send the right messages to the right people, only members of the room will get the messages for that particular room.

To check for messages or when the user leaves the room, we use event handlers on socket. Every communication over Socket.IO is classed as a message, not to be confused with the messages that are written in the chatroom. Sending messages is called *emitting*. For messages in the chatroom to be sent to each other, we first emit the message on the client side (which I will get to shortly) to the server, which then sends it to the other clients connected to the room. To emit a message to the room from the server we use io.sockets.in(room).emit(key, value);. For a chatroom message we use the string 'message' as the key and the data is passed through as the value from a data parameter on the event listener. For leaving a room, the key is 'leave'.

```
io.sockets.on('connection', function (socket) {
    var room = socket.handshake.headers.referer;
    socket.join(room);
    socket.on('message', function (data) {
        io.sockets.in(room).emit('message', data);
    });
    socket.on('leave', function (room) {
        socket.leave(room);
    });
});
```

And that's it for the server in terms of a basic chatroom, you can see how brief the code is in Listing 7-1. All we need to do now is for the event handlers on the client-side to emit the messages when sent so that, using the power of Socket.IO rooms and the code we have just written, it will automatically send the messages to anybody in the same room— in real time! There is no AJAX or long polling to worry about, Socket.IO uses the best method available (most modern browsers use Web Sockets but others fall back to the appropriate method). The lack of using AJAX is one of the biggest factors in my choice to not use jQuery or any similar libraries for this chapter, though you may need to for larger projects.

Listing 7-1.

```
<script>
    var socket = io.connect('http://localhost');

    socket.on('message', function(evt) {
        document.querySelector("#messages").innerHTML += '<p><span class="nickname">'
+evt.nickname+': </span><span class="message">' + evt.message +'</span></p>';
    });

    sendButton = document.querySelector("#send");
    var messages = document.querySelector("#message");
    sendButton.addEventListener('click', function() {

        socket.emit('message', {
          "message": messages.value,
          "nickname": document.querySelector("#nickname").value || 'Guest'
        });

        messages.value = "";
    });
</script>
```

▓ **Note**   To use Socket.IO on the client-side you must include `<script src="/socket.io/socket.io.js"></script>` although you do not need to worry about the location because Node.js deals with it automatically.

Summary

Many Node.js beginners always feel a bit daunted at the prospect of learning a technology that is so different from what they are used to. I hope this chapter has eased you in to the world of Node.js in such a way that you find it almost laughably easy to make a real-time multi-user application. Chatrooms can be very diverse, so this exercise should give you a great starting point to learn more of the language. You can take it further by enhancing your chatroom using features of the language that you find interesting. In the next chapter we will be adding video and audio streaming to the chatroom as a conference-style feature that will take you to the next level of node expertise.

CHAPTER 8

Video-to-Video Using WebRTC

The natural progression to our chatroom is video-to-video, such as the kind Skype and Google Hangouts use, but until very recently this was a lot harder than it sounds. Why? Yep, you guessed it . . . plugins were required (namely, Flash). It was not until 2012, nearly 20 years after the start of the Web, that the beginnings of native video streaming from a webcam started trickling into the browsers. Now that WebRTC is starting to become well supported, it is worth learning how to use it. I am not going to pretend it is simple—it isn't—but, once you've got your head around how it works, it does make sense.

Introduction to WebRTC

Okay, so we know that WebRTC is used to allow communication between browsers, but what is it? WebRTC is actually a set of specifications that are often used together to create a real-time communication link. The group of specs includes one for data too so it is not just for video and audio (though at the time of writing, the data spec is not well supported but it is being actively developed). WebRTC is formed very similar to TCP servers in that it requires a handshake sent using correct protocols rather than just being a common API that you are used to using. It should also be noted that WebRTC is peer to peer rather than client/server, which is why it requires extra networking on the client-side. Since the majority of web developers have probably never needed to write a TCP server, I think we should start from the beginning.

GetUserMedia()

One of the hardest problems with creating native video communication before WebRTC was not the fact that communication itself was hard to do (though without any peer to peer capabilities, it was very hard to do). No, the most difficult problem was accessing the webcam!

Luckily, we now have `navigator.getUserMedia()`, which is a method that lets us get both the video and audio from an input device and do something with it using the callback.

```
navigator.getUserMedia( {audio: true, video: true},
    function(s) {
        vid.src = URL.createObjectURL(s);
        vid.play();
    }, function(error) {throw error;}
);
```

The first parameter is a configuration object that let's you choose the type of input that you want to use. Then we have two callbacks, the first for what to do if the input successfully gives you a stream and the second for if it fails.

And that's that. Simple, right? One of the most annoying problems in web development, now possible using just one method.

Now, while we are talking purely about getUserMedia, I would like to point out that you could do anything with it that you can do with a normal video (since it goes through the video element). In the next few chapters we will be looking at computer vision, a massive topic that is not usually thought of as related to the Web, we will be using getUserMedia as the base for the entire project and it will show you that video is not just for conference calls.

Specifications

As I mentioned at the beginning of the chapter, WebRTC is a set of specifications. It consists of the following three APIs:

- Media Stream API

- PeerConnection API

- DataChannel API

The Media Stream API primarily covers the getUserMedia() method that I explained previously. It requires its own specification because, despite being very easy to use, it is complicated for browser implementers. Peer Connections are also complicated because there has never before been any kind of peer-to-peer networking within the HTML APIs. It provides us with a simple API to use rather than getting bogged down in the messy workings of networking.

Using the API, we create a Peer Connection object to handle all peer-to-peer communication. This object consists of an ICE (Interactive Connectivity Establishment) agent, the state of the connection, and an ICE state. Luckily for us, this is handled using the API too! So instead of working out the correct states and so on, we can simply create the object using new RTCIceCandidate and it handles the states itself.

The Data Channel API is, at the time of writing, the least implemented due to it being much easier to transfer simple data already (using servers) than it is to transfer video and audio in real time. Data channels will probably be more important than the media streams because the data channels allow data to be sent peer to peer, which has countless possibilities such as for making multiplayer games that do not need a server (or at least, the server does not need to take the full load). As we will see in the chapters that follow, the media streams can be extremely powerful but data has a lot more common usages, so it is exciting to be able to transfer data without a server!

Servers

I'm sorry. Yes, WebRTC does not need servers—but it does. If you think about it on very simple terms, you always need a way to find each other. Without a server, unless you manually enter the IP addresses, the Peer Connections simply cannot know where to connect. So we use servers, in our case Node.js, so that messages get to the right clients. This is known as signaling. The complexity of the servers depends on your needs. We will be writing a fairly basic server that handles offers and candidates but will be limited to two clients. It would be fairly simple to extend the server to enable more connections. I encourage you to attempt this, as it is a great way to understand the intricacies of WebRTC and its networking structure.

Where to Start?

As you can see, we have quite a big task ahead of us. I think we should start with the server because it is the smallest part of the code and acts as a kind of testing suite for us. We are extending the code from Chapter 7, which I have included here for your memory and as a comparison.

```
var app = require('express')(),
server = require('http').createServer(app),
io = require('socket.io').listen(server);
io.set('log level', 1); // Removes debug logs
server.listen(8080);
```

```
app.get('/:id', function (req, res) {
    res.sendfile(__dirname + '/index.html');
});

io.sockets.on('connection', function (socket) {
    var room = socket.handshake.headers.referer;
    socket.join(room);
    socket.on('message', function (data) {
        io.sockets.in(room).emit('message', data);
    });
    socket.on('leave', function (room) {
        socket.leave(room);
    });
});
```

We need to keep all this, though some parts will be edited. In applications such as this, where there is potential for it to be quite complicated, I tend to give each socket a unique identifier. To do this I have used node-uuid, so we need to import that at the top. Then within the code that runs when a new socket has connected, we assign the output of uuid.v1() to socket.id. Of course we need to let the client know that it has been given an id, so we emit an 'assigned_id' message that sends the id to the client.

```
var express = require('express'),
    http = require('http'),
    uuid = require ("node-uuid"),
    app = express(),
    server = http.createServer(app),
    io = require('socket.io').listen(server);

io.sockets.on('connection', function (socket) {

    var room = socket.handshake.headers.referer;
    console.log('JOINED', room);
    socket.join(room);
    socket.id = uuid.v1();

    socket.emit('assigned_id', socket.id);

    // Everything else goes here
});
```

The client-side needs to look for the emitted message and to store it within the client-side socket.

```
socket.on('assigned_id', function(data)  {
  console.log('assigned id' + data);
  socket.id = data;
});
```

Now we need to create the structure for the signaling. It starts when a client's webcam is successfully running, it adds its stream to its own peer connection, then creates an offer. Within the callback, the peer connection is given the local description. We get the description from the callback as a parameter. This description holds all the data (as SDP) about the client, such as IP address. I will explain the exact format of the description after we have written the server; it is mostly complicated data for the browser but some of it is useful to know about. The client now needs to let the server know that it is time to send the offer to the other client. To avoid confusion, let's call the original client c1 and the one it connects to c2. So, the server needs to send any 'received_offer' messages on to the correct socket, c2. It eventually does the same for both 'received_candidate' and 'received_answer' as well; these three are all that are needed for basic switching.

```
socket.on('received_offer', function(data) {
    console.log("received_offer %j", data);
    io.sockets.in(room).emit('received_offer', data);
});

socket.on('received_candidate', function(data) {
  console.log(" received_candidate %j", data);
  io.sockets.in(room).emit('received_candidate', data);
});

socket.on('received_answer', function(data) {
  console.log(" received_answer %j", data);
  io.sockets.in(room).emit('received_answer', data);
});
```

You must remember that the entire code runs on both clients, so c1 will send received_offer to c2 but c2 will also send it to c1. This is how we know when both are ready. When c2 receives the offer it sets its peer connection's remote description to the one that c1 sent (c1's local description becomes c2's remote description and vice versa). It then creates an answer that sends back its local description (again, from the callback); this step may not seem necessary since they both already have each other's description but it can be considered a confirmation. It also sets a Boolean variable, on the client-side, called connected to be true so that this cannot repeat itself and cause an infinite loop. The peer connection, on each client, registers that an ICE candidate is ready once the local descriptions are set; this triggers an event that is handled by the client using pc.onIceCandidate(), which is then used to send more data (in the form of SDP, which I shall explain soon) to the server by emitting the 'received_candidate' message that was mentioned previously. Of course, c2 now receives the SDP and uses it to add c1 as an ICE candidate to the peer connection.

If all went to according to plan, c1 and c2 will now see each other. Well, they would if we had implemented the client-side. My explanation may have seemed quite confusing but that is because I wanted to explain exactly how it works, not just that the server needs to serve a few messages. It is basically the same concept as we had in Chapter 7 and a pattern that you will often use when writing node.js code. Listing 8-1 is the code for the server, including a message for closing the connection smoothly and another for how many clients are in the room:

Listing 8-1. Server.js

```
var express = require('express'),
    http = require('http'),
    uuid = require ("node-uuid"),
    app = express(),
    server = http.createServer(app),
    io = require('socket.io').listen(server);
io.set('log level', 1); // Removes debug logs
app.use(express.static('public'));
server.listen(8080);

app.get('/:id?', function (req, res) {
    res.sendfile(__dirname + '/index.html');
});
```

```
io.sockets.on('connection', function(socket) {
    var room = socket.handshake.headers.referer;
    console.log('JOINED', room);
    socket.join(room);
    socket.id = uuid.v1();

    socket.emit('assigned_id', socket.id);

    socket.on('debug_clients', function(data) {
        socket.emit('room_count', io.sockets.manager.rooms['/' + room].length);
    });

    io.sockets.in(room).emit('room_count', io.sockets.manager.rooms['/' + room].length);

    socket.on('received_offer', function(data) {
        console.log(" received_offer %j", data);
        io.sockets.in(room).emit('received_offer', data);
    });

    socket.on('received_candidate', function(data) {
        console.log(" received_candidate %j", data);
        io.sockets.in(room).emit('received_candidate', data);
    });

    socket.on('received_answer', function(data) {
        console.log(" received_answer %j", data);
        io.sockets.in(room).emit('received_answer', data);
    });

    socket.on('close', function() {
        console.log("closed %j", room);
        io.sockets.in(room).emit('closed', room);
    });

});
```

Technologies Behind WebRTC

Okay, let's take a brief break from the code. I've described the flow of how WebRTC clients connect to each other, but there are a lot of terms that you probably haven't seen before. So before we write the client-side code, I would like to go through the technologies behind WebRTC and how they work, they are a bit out of scope for this book so I encourage you to read more about them. If you're not particularly interested, then feel free to skip over to the next section where we implement the client-side.

ICE

I've mentioned ICE quite a bit. It stands for *Interactive Connectivity Establishment*, which according to RFC 5245 (http://www.ietf.org/rfc/rfc5245.txt) is "A Protocol for Network Address Translator (NAT) Traversal for Offer/Answer Protocols". The RFC goes into a lot of detail, which some of you may find very interesting, but I think the abstract sums up the purpose quite well. To some of you this will sound like absolute gobbledygook, so hopefully once you have read my brief summaries about ICE and the other technologies then you will understand it.

This document describes a protocol for Network Address Translator (NAT) traversal for UDP-based multimedia sessions established with the offer/answer model. This protocol is called Interactive Connectivity Establishment (ICE). ICE makes use of the Session Traversal Utilities for NAT (STUN) protocol and its extension, Traversal Using Relay NAT (TURN). ICE can be used by any protocol utilizing the offer/answer model, such as the Session Initiation Protocol (SIP).

RFC 5245 Abstract

As I explained in the "Specifications" section of this chapter, the peer connection that every WebRTC client must have is made up of components, including `iceConnectionState`, `iceGatheringState` and the ICE Agent. The ICE Agent is the important (yet simple) part. It is the endpoint for WebRTC on each client and it is responsible for communicating with the other endpoints, using a signaling protocol. The reason we use ICE at all is that it is (as the abstract states) a standardized protocol for NAT traversal for UDP communication. This basically means that it is a way of getting through security, such as firewalls, without being blocked. ICE works by checking all possible paths of communication in parallel, which quickly finds the best possible path. The states are used (quite obviously) to find the state of the ICE Agent and they are read-only.

The possible states of `iceGatheringState` are

- new

- gathering

- complete

The possible states of `iceConnectionState` are

- starting

- checking

- connected

- completed

- failed

- disconnected

- closed

NAT Traversal

NAT is the technology behind hardware routers (and some commercial switches) that allows many machines behind one router to work using one IP. It takes incoming packets of data, and sends them to the correct device based on where it came from. It translates the internal network addresses (for example, 192.168.1.123) to the outward facing IP and back again. Inbound communication is restricted for many reasons, including security, and usually involves a port whitelist table that the NAT device uses to associate internal addresses to inbound ports (commonly referred to as a *firewall*).

NAT Traversal is a name for a group of methods of getting around this in a user friendly way. Without NAT Traversal techniques, users would have to manually open ports on their firewall to allow inbound traffic, and give this port information to other connecting parties. Some common NAT Traversal techniques are; Reverse Proxies, Socket Secure (SOCKS), Universal Plug and Play (UPnP), and UDP Hole Punching.

STUN/TURN

STUN (Session Traversal Utilities for NAT) and TURN (Traversal Using Relays around NAT) are both signaling protocols that are often used as tools by ICE for the NAT traversal. There are open source implementations for each if you wish to run your own server. The two that I used for this chapter (you only need one, but you can have an array of them so that there are backups) are run by Google and Mozilla at `stun:stun.l.google.com:19302` and `stun:stun.services.mozilla.com`. You will notice that both of these servers are STUN. This is mostly because they were the first free servers that I found to be reliable. The main difference between the two is that TURN uses a relay technique, so the data is relayed through to server to get to the client. The upside however is that TURN builds on STUN, so it always tries to use STUN first but if that fails it, then relays. Another advantage of TURN is that it works with Symmetric NATs, which STUN does not.

SDP

If I called the abstract for the ICE protocol gobbledygook, then my vocabulary cannot describe SDP. At first glance (and probably at second and third too), it looks impenetrable. But do not worry, the important bits are quite simple to understand and the rest is documented (primarily in RFC4566). SDP stands for Session Description Protocol and is the form of data that is sent between clients. Below is an example of SDP, in this case running the code for this chapter under localhost and having a connection between two Google Chrome tabs. There is a wide range of possible SDP contents, largely dependent on the stage of communication, so don't expect it to look identical if you look at your own SDP data. I have only included the first 11 lines because the majority of it is not often useful to us for debugging and it mostly concerned with encryption.

```
v=0
o=- 68883115068875211333 2 IN IP4 127.0.0.1
s=-
t=0 0
a=group:BUNDLE audio video
a=msid-semantic: WMS YuWoij3TGBXItoUd2iqCWMbt7FnkBqSNpP96
m=audio 1 RTP/SAVPF 111 103 104 0 8 107 106 105 13 126
c=IN IP4 0.0.0.0
a=rtcp:1 IN IP4 0.0.0.0
a=ice-ufrag:qbj6LYoXCSHnUUuq
a=ice-pwd:C/eziXfWhziBTVpMylTLU2M3
```

Daunting, I know. Let's start with the letters before the equal sign. This is called the type and it is always just one character and is case-sensitive. The order of types is predefined, mostly to reduce errors and so that parsers can be implemented more easily. Of course it is also handy for debugging, as we will always know where the data we are looking for should be! I will only explain the first four lines as they are the ones that are most likely to go wrong, the rest are optional and therefore are less likely to break (and if it does, more likely to be a bug in the browser rather than your code). Do note that the attributes are in the form of `<type>=<attribute>:<value>`. Most attributes are easily searchable online if you are interested in learning about them, and I will probably write an article to accompany this chapter on my site.

```
Session description
   v= (protocol version)
   o= (originator and session identifier)
   s= (session name)
   i=* (session information)
   u=* (URI of description)
   e=* (email address)
```

```
p=* (phone number)
c=* (connection information -- not required if included in
     all media)
b=* (zero or more bandwidth information lines)
One or more time descriptions ("t=" and "r=" lines; see below)
z=* (time zone adjustments)
k=* (encryption key)
a=* (zero or more session attribute lines)
Zero or more media descriptions

Time description
   t=  (time the session is active)
   r=* (zero or more repeat times)

Media description, if present
   m=  (media name and transport address)
   i=* (media title)
   c=* (connection information -- optional if included at
        session level)
   b=* (zero or more bandwidth information lines)
   k=* (encryption key)
   a=* (zero or more media attribute lines)
* means optional
```

This guide to types was taken from the RFC 4566, so credit goes to The Internet Society. You can see quite easily how the SDP object breaks up into three sections. At the time of writing, all SDP objects start with v=0 because there are no other versions available. In my example, the second line (originator and session identifier) was o=- 6888311506875211333 2 IN IP4 127.0.0.1. The hyphen indicates that there is no username because I was not using a private TURN server. The long number is the unique identifier for the session. Next we find the important part of this line, at least for debugging, the session version; this is the amount of times the session data has changed (each time we send a new message with data, this number increments). You can use the session version to be absolutely sure that the session description was updated. IN stands for Internet, it is there to make the protocol future proof. We then have the type of IP, in this case IP version 4. Last on the second line is the IP address. I was running locally so it reported the IP address back as being 127.0.0.1 (localhost).

You may notice that my example jumps straight to the timing section, this is an implementation decision (in this case by Chrome) as the lines in between are all optional. The first 0 represents start time and the following 0 represents stop time. Since both are 0, it means the session is permanent.

Client-side Code

Okay, that was a nice break from the code but I think we are all ready to dive back in with a firmer understanding of how WebRTC actually works and what the data we are sending really is. Remember the walkthrough of how the signaling works? Here it is again in the form of a list to make it easier to implement:

1. Start webcam.

2. Add stream to peer connection.

3. Send received_offer message with Local Description.

   a. Add local description to Peer Connection.

4. Adds received description to Peer Connection as Remote Description.

5. Create Answer.

6. Set connect to true to prevent infinite loop.

7. Add ICE Candidate.

8. Load webcam.

You may remember from the beginning of the chapter that the correct way to start the webcam is by using `navigator.getUserMedia()`, unfortunately due to the different implementations in browsers at the time of writing we are using `Adapter.js` and that drops the vendor prefix in order to get RTC working cross browser. To make the video load quickly, without worrying about user interfaces and so on. we put `getUserMedia` into a function called `broadcast()` and call it without `window.onload`. Within the callback of `getUserMedia`, we need to add the stream to the Peer Connection, then use `URL.createObjectURL()` (which we used in Chapter 2) to add the stream to the video element and play the video. Once the server sends a message that the room count is more than 1, it is time to send an offer to the server.

```
var socket = io.connect('http://localhost');
var pc = new RTCPeerConnection(servers, mediaConstraints);
var initConnection = false;

socket.on('room_count', function(data)  {
  room_count = data;
  console.log('ROOM COUNT', data);
  if (room_count > 1)
    initConnection = true;
});

function broadcast() {
  getUserMedia({audio: true, video: true}, function(s) {
    pc.addStream(s);
    console.log("GOT MEDIA");
    vid1.src = URL.createObjectURL(s);
    vid1.play();
    if (initConnection) start();
  }, function(error) {throw error;});
};

window.onload = function() {
  broadcast();
};
```

Within `start()` we need to create the offer, this happens through Peer Connection's `pc.createOffer()`. The method itself provides the SDP accessible as a parameter, we can then use it to set the local description and emit a `'received_offer'` message to the server containing the SDP.

```
function start() {
  console.log('STARTING');
  // this initializes the peer connection
  pc.createOffer(function(description) {
    console.log(description);
```

```
      pc.setLocalDescription(description);
      socket.emit('received_offer', JSON.stringify(description));
  }, null, mediaConstraints);
};
```

You will notice two extra parameters, the second is a callback used for error handling (for simplicity I have left that out) and the third is a variable that I've called mediaConstraints. This variable contains both mandatory data that says whether video and/or audio is available as well as optional, in this case DtlsSrtpKeyAgreement, which is used to enable Datagram Transport Layer Security for browsers that do not enable it by default (such as older versions of Chrome).

```
var mediaConstraints = {
  'mandatory': {
    'OfferToReceiveAudio':true,
    'OfferToReceiveVideo':true
  },
  'optional': [{'DtlsSrtpKeyAgreement': 'true'}]
};
```

This brings us to step 4, adding the remote description to the Peer Connection. We get this description from the "received_offer" message, the one that we previously sent (remember that both client 1 and 2 send the message to each other). This starts by parsing the stringifyed JSON of the SDP and store in a variable called data. We then check that the data is definitely an offer by accessing the type property, just as a way to prevent possible edge cases. Then we set the peer connection's remote description to be an RTCSessionDescription of the data. With that done, we use peer connection's createAnswer() in much the same way as we used createOffer(). First set the local description to be the same as the data that is provided, then emit a "received_answer" message to the server.

```
socket.on('received_offer', function(data) {
  data = JSON.parse(data);
  console.log('received offer');
  if (data.type == "offer")  {
    pc.setRemoteDescription(new RTCSessionDescription(data));
    pc.createAnswer(function(data) {
      console.log('sending answer', data);
      pc.setLocalDescription(data);
      socket.emit('received_answer', data );
    }, null, mediaConstraints);
  }
});
```

Of course, we now check for "received_answer" (this all gets much less complicated as you break it down into pieces, don't you think?). We now need a variable called connected so that it only attempts to connect once, if the variable is set to false and the data is definitely an answer, then we once again create a remote description using the SDP that is then added to the peer connection. Then we simply set connected to true so that it doesn't keep reconnecting (again, an edge case that shouldn't often happen).

```
socket.on('received_answer', function(data) {
  console.log('received answer', data);
  if(!connected && data.type == "answer") {
    var description = new RTCSessionDescription(data);
```

```
    console.log("Setting remote description", description);
    pc.setRemoteDescription(description);
    connected = true;
  }
});
```

The peer connection now knows that it had an ICE candidate as the peer connection 'gathers candidates' once the local descriptions have been set. When it has an ICE candidate, we then send its own candidate back (including an id and label) as a "received_candidate" message. So we now need to listen for "received_candidate" and add that candidate to the peer connection. This process is mostly just for confirmation of each candidate, it is more of a problem when there are more than two clients. Listing 8-2 shows the current state of the client.js file.

Listing 8-2. Client.js

```
socket.on('received_candidate', function(data) {
  console.log('received candidate', data);
  data = JSON.parse(data);

  var candidate = new RTCIceCandidate({
    sdpMLineIndex: data.label,
    candidate: data.candidate
  });
  pc.addIceCandidate(candidate);
});

pc.onicecandidate = function(e) {
  console.log("oniceCandidate", e);
  if(e.candidate) {
    socket.emit('received_candidate', JSON.stringify({
        label: e.candidate.sdpMLineIndex,
        id: e.candidate.sdpMid,
        candidate: e.candidate.candidate
    }));
  }
};
```

Now that both peer connections have all the candidates needed, we are practically finished. Once everything is ready, the addstream event will be triggered, letting us put the remote video stream into a video element (in this case, vid2).

```
pc.onaddstream = function(e) {
  console.log('start remote video stream');
  console.log(e);
  vid2.src = URL.createObjectURL(e.stream);
  vid2.play();
};
```

It is worth noting that the user who has not closed the connection will see the remote video as frozen on the last frame that was delivered, you could instead make it say that the connection has dropped by having an event handler on the 'close' message. The final version of the code can be found in the download available on the Apress website at www.apress.com/9781430259442 or on my own website at shanehudson.net/javascript-creativity.

Summary

I hope you enjoyed this chapter, WebRTC is one of those technologies that are quite confusing at first and is very complex at a browser implementation level (such as the SDP), but once you get your head around it, it is actually fairly simple. It is also incredibly powerful. We did the most obvious use-case here, because it is the most useful as an introduction, but WebRTC is (especially if you want to drop the signaling and have a different method of finding other clients) useful as a general usage peer to peer technology; for example, you could have a game or a prototype app in which you want to have users connected without the overheads of a server. The access to the user's webcam is also extremely powerful, as you will see in the next chapter where we start to explore the realm of Computer Vision.

CHAPTER 9

Motion Detection

An Introduction to Motion Detection

Throughout the book so far we have looked at a number of technologies that have obvious applications that you can implement without too much creativity, things that may not have been possible before but that are not too hard to do now, such as the video-to-video chat in the previous chapter. I would now like to delve into the realms of computer vision, one of my personal interests and one that has a large variety of ways to apply it. Because this book is neither about advanced computer vision nor targeted at academia/research labs, we will stick to relatively naïve algorithms and avoid any artificial intelligence that requires training, such as facial recognition.

In this chapter we focus on motion detection, because it ties in well with the WebRTC and is probably the most useful aspect of basic computer vision. In the next chapter we will be creating a musical instrument that can be played using motion detection and with other people over WebRTC, which should nicely tie the entire book together. For now though, think about the other kinds of applications you could use motion detection for, such as home security or even just visual effects.

Boilerplate for Video Manipulation

As you will have noticed by now, most of these kinds of projects follow a similar pattern. Here I quickly go over the pattern that we will be using for video manipulation for the majority (if not all) the code in this chapter. We start with a shim for `window.URL` and `navigator.getUserMedia`, for this chapter I've decided to use a variable that uses the method that is compatible with the browser rather than using a full polyfill as we did in the previous chapter (because the full WebRTC stack is less supported than getUserMedia).

```
window.URL = window.URL || window.webkitURL;
navigator.getUserMedia  =  navigator.getUserMedia ||
                           navigator.webkitGetUserMedia ||
                           navigator.mozGetUserMedia ||
                           navigator.msGetUserMedia;
if (navigator.getUserMedia === undefined) {
    throw new Error("Browser doesn't support getUserMedia");
}
```

Now we need to set up the page, in this case so that both the video and canvas elements are full size within the browser window. Just set the video element to autoplay, get the context of the canvas, and initialize the video stream. To draw the frame we connect the stream and add an event listener that calls draw() once the video is ready (for example, 'canplay'). There is now a slight problem, normally this would work fine but some versions of Firefox (all of which at the time of writing are quite commonly used) have a bug that causes drawImage to run before the size of the video frame has been set. The error is NS_ERROR_NOT_AVAILABLE and to prevent it we can use a try catch. Of course, in production code it is recommended to do thorough error handling anyway, so this should not be too much of a problem.

Within the try catch block, we need to draw the image from the video element to the canvas context. To get data that we can manipulate we need to get the frame using `ctx.getImageData(0, 0, w, h)`, which has a data property that can be used to retrieve and modify the frame. Following is the boilerplate code. Note that there is a comment showing where to manipulate the data.

```
function setup() {
  videoElement = document.querySelector("video");
  videoElement.width = w = window.innerWidth;
  videoElement.height = h = window.innerHeight;
  videoElement.autoplay = true;

  canvas = document.querySelector('canvas');
  canvas.width = w;
  canvas.height = h;
  ctx = canvas.getContext('2d');

  navigator.getUserMedia({video: true}, function (stream) {
      videoElement.src = window.URL.createObjectURL(stream);
      videoElement.addEventListener('canplay', draw);
  }, function() {});
}

function draw() {
  if (videoElement.paused || videoElement.ended) {
      return;
  }
  try {
      ctx.drawImage(videoElement, 0, 0, w, h);
      manip = ctx.getImageData(0, 0, w, h);
      var data = manip.data;

      // Manipulate the frame by modifying data

      ctx.putImageData(manip, 0, 0);
      requestAnimationFrame(draw);
  }
  catch (e) {
      if (e.name == "NS_ERROR_NOT_AVAILABLE") {
          setTimeout(draw, 0);
      }
      else {
          throw e;
      }
  }
}
```

Basic Video Manipulation

You should remember that back in Chapter 3 we manipulated video by simply iterating over the pixels, but because that was at the beginning of the book I will quickly go over it again. This time, let's just invert the pixels so that we can easily see how the manipulation works without worrying about the exact algorithm used to create an effect.

The function for inverting the frame is invertFrame and take data as a parameter, the call to invertFrame should be placed where the comment was in the boilerplate code and the data parameter should come from the data variable. Do note that we will be returning the data variable so that it directly effects the manip.data from the boilerplate code (since this is the actual frame). We start with the data in the form of a Uint8ClampedArray. This means that the array contains unsigned ints (that is, positive numbers) and they are clamped to 8 bits (a byte) and because 2^8 is 256, the max number in any index of the array is 255 (due, of course, to counting from 0).

▓ **Note**   The array is comprised of RGBA colors, so you should iterate over every four indexes to get the start of each color.

So while we iterate over the array, we start from the beginning of each color and therefore need to (usually, unless you just want to find red) check the indexes of the green and blue colors as well (by checking data[i+1] and data[i+2], respectively). To invert the colors, we need to minus the current value of each color from 255 (for example, making white become black).

```
function invertFrame(data)  {

    // Iterate through each pixel, inverting it
    for (var i = 0; i < data.length; i += 4) {
        var r = data[i],
            g = data[i+1],
            b = data[i+2];
        data[i] = 255 - r;
        data[i+1] = 255 - g;
        data[i+2] = 255 - b;
    }

    return data;
}
```

See Listing 9-1 for how this fits with the boilerplate code.

Listing 9-1.

```
window.URL = window.URL || window.webkitURL;
navigator.getUserMedia  =   navigator.getUserMedia ||
                            navigator.webkitGetUserMedia ||
                            navigator.mozGetUserMedia ||
                            navigator.msGetUserMedia;
if (navigator.getUserMedia === undefined) {
    throw new Error("Browser doesn't support getUserMedia");
}
```

```
var videoElement, canvas, ctx, manip, w, h;

window.addEventListener('DOMContentLoaded', setup);

function setup() {
    videoElement = document.querySelector("video");
    videoElement.width = w = window.innerWidth;
    videoElement.height = h = window.innerHeight;
    videoElement.autoplay = true;

    canvas = document.querySelector('canvas');
    canvas.width = w;
    canvas.height = h;
    ctx = canvas.getContext('2d');

    navigator.getUserMedia({video: true}, function (stream) {
        videoElement.src = window.URL.createObjectURL(stream);
        videoElement.addEventListener('canplay', draw);
    }, function() {});
}

function draw() {
    if (videoElement.paused || videoElement.ended) {
        return;
    }
    try {
        ctx.drawImage(videoElement, 0, 0, w, h);
        manip = ctx.getImageData(0, 0, w, h);
        var data = manip.data;

        data = invertFrame(data);

        ctx.putImageData(manip, 0, 0);
        requestAnimationFrame(draw);
    }
    catch (e) {
        if (e.name == "NS_ERROR_NOT_AVAILABLE") {
            setTimeout(draw, 0);
        }
        else {
            throw e;
        }
    }
}

function invertFrame(data) {

    // Iterate through each pixel, inverting it
    for (var i = 0; i < data.length; i += 4) {
        var r = data[i],
            g = data[i+1],
            b = data[i+2];
```

```
        data[i] = 255 - r;
        data[i+1] = 255 - g;
        data[i+2] = 255 - b;
    }

    return data;
}
```

Motion Detection

Now that you have refreshed knowledge of manipulating video, let's dive into our first demonstration of using detecting motion in the video. This is a computer vision that is useful despite (in this case) being completely naïve, there is no artificial intelligence involved nor particularly complicated algorithms. If you think about it, motion detection is simply showing the difference between frames. We could make it more complicated by optimizing it, detect over a number of frames or to track the motion, but for now let's just find the difference.

It is quite easy to do this; you take the current data and store it so that on the next frame you have both new data and old data. Once you have both pieces of data, you can compare the two and find the pixels that are different. However, if you do this, you will soon notice that the camera doesn't see everything the same each frame so it will look like there is a lot of motion in the background. To get around this, you can use a threshold to alter the accuracy. Because we are not using any artificial intelligence, this can be an arbitrary number that works well (15 worked well while I was testing). In Figure 9-1, you can see the motion of my head as a result of the arbitrary threshold that I used. If we were creating an AI, it would attempt to find the most likely pixels to be the kind of motion we are looking for, such as the outline of a hand or more simply a bunch of pixels rather than a single movement (since nothing we will be interested in is the size of a pixel!).

Figure 9-1. *A screenshot showing the rough outline of my face being detected as I move*

Within the try block, we slightly modify the boilerplate code so that it checks oldData for being null (which should be its initial value), if it isn't, then it manipulates and if it is null, then it assigns the current data from data.manip.

```
bctx.drawImage(videoElement, 0, 0, w, h);
manip = bctx.getImageData(0, 0, w, h);
var data = manip.data;
if (oldData != null) {
    data = motionDetection(data, oldData);
    ctx.putImageData(manip, 0, 0);
    oldData = null;
}
else  {
    oldData = manip.data;
}


requestAnimationFrame(draw);
```

The motionDetection function works as explained previously; it takes both the current frame's data and the previous (although this could be optimized or more advanced in a variety of ways, so it is not necessarily only the previous frame), then compares them and draws a red pixel to every pixel that has moved and is within the bounds of the threshold.

```
function motionDetection(data, oldData)  {

    // Iterate through each pixel, changing to 255 if it has not changed
    for( var y = 0 ; y < h; y++ ) {
        for( var x = 0 ; x < w; x++ ) {
            var indexOld = (y * w + x) * 4,
                    oldr = oldData[indexOld],
                    oldg = oldData[indexOld+1],
                    oldb = oldData[indexOld+2],
                    olda = oldData[indexOld+3];
            var indexNew = (y * w + x) * 4,
                    r = data[indexNew],
                    g = data[indexNew+1],
                    b = data[indexNew+2],
                    a = data[indexNew+3];

            if (oldr > r - 15 || oldg > g - 15 || oldb > b - 15)
            {
                data[indexNew] = 255;
                data[indexNew+1] = 255;
                data[indexNew+2] = 255;
                data[indexNew+3] = 255;
                detected = true;
            }
```

```
        else
        {
            data[indexNew] = 255;
            data[indexNew+1] = 0;
            data[indexNew+2] = 0;
            data[indexNew+3] = 255;
        }
    }
}

    return data;
}
```

Motion Tracking

Okay, so detecting motion is one thing but, unless you are creating an alarm system or making art, it isn't very useful alone. You usually want to either make the computer clever enough to recognize what the object is (especially true for robots) or, more often, just know where the same object is—this is called tracking. We produced an image that shows motion but it doesn't make any attempt to group the motion as an object. There are a large variety of ways to do this, such as calibrating based on color and looking for areas with the correct average color, or you could use artificial intelligence and actually train it to look for an object.

While color calibration is easier than using AI, it can cause a lot of problems and the math soon becomes far too complicated, for just a chapter of a book, if you want it to be reliable. So instead we are going to go half way between the two methods and use library called js-objectDetect (written by Martin Tschirsich and found on github at `https://github.com/mtschirs/js-objectdetect`), which is based on the OpenCV object detector and can take already trained classifiers. Before we get to the code, let's look into how the library actually works.

Haar-like Features

Most image processing algorithms require a way to detect features in an image and there are quite a few different ways to do that. The most common (due to their use in the Viola-Jones algorithm) are called Haar-like features. These are based on the original Haar wavelets that were proposed by Alfréd Haar in 1909. A *wavelet* is a mathematical function that cuts data into different frequencies, then it scales and analyzes the data for patterns. It is an essential tool for signal processing and provides an alternative, with the advantage of being able to scale the data, to the Fourier transform (which we used in Chapter 3). Haar-like features can be considered as a more tangible form of Haar wavelets, as you can visualize them using different sized black and white rectangles (as shown in Figure 9-2).

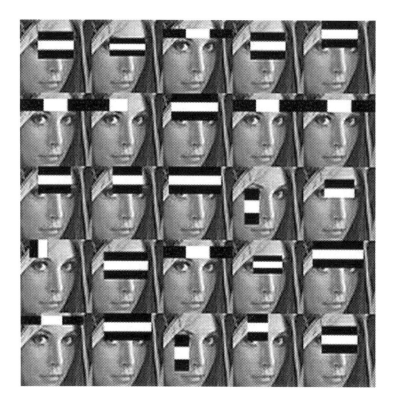

Figure 9-2. An example of Haar-like features, visualized as black and white rectangles

The reason they are black and white rectangles, as opposed to something that resembles the feature they are searching for, is that most objects have a common pattern of shadows (such as between an eye and nose). They work efficiently by using summed area tables, to produce what is known as an integral image, which allows quick lookups of the sum of all the pixels in the rectangle without needing to calculate them every time. On their own, Haar-like features are not particularly useful but when you use them as part of the Viola-Jones algorithm (which uses a moving window to search) then they become essential.

Viola–Jones

As you probably guessed from the previous section, the algorithm that powers both js-objectDetect and the OpenCV object detector is based on a paper written by Paul Viola and Michael Jones in 2001 (later improved on by Rainer Lienhart) and commonly known simply as Viola-Jones. I will not go into details about the algorithm, as it is quite complicated, but if you have a deep interest in computer vision or artificial intelligence, then it may be worth reading. The original paper does include some rather advanced math but it is written in a way that shouldn't be too difficult to understand. The algorithm basically works by taking two sets of images, positive matches and negative; these are used to train it by going over each image with a small window that attempts to match the contents of the window of the image to Haar-like features. As with all training, the larger the sets, the more accurate it should be.

The paper described the algorithm as being a "visual object detection framework", so it can be implemented in a variety of different ways. The paper is comprised of three main contributions, which can be considered as the main components of any Viola-Jones–based facial detection algorithm. The first component is integral images, which as I explained earlier, is how Haar-like features are so efficient. The second component is a learning algorithm based on AdaBoost. The last component that they put forward as being important to facial detection is cascade classifiers, which are used to quickly discard the background of the image. It is quite interesting to note that the algorithm used for detection is the same as the one used for training, so there is no extra step required to actually use the classifiers. The classifiers are the outcomes of the training and we will be using predefined cascades so that training is not required (because it needs a large data set and can take a long time). The js-objectDetect library includes some classifiers as samples (including mouth, eye, and hand classifiers, not just faces), so we shall be using those for this chapter. There are two types of cascade classifier, stump and tree. A stump is a single node of a tree and is usually best to use due to the balance between accuracy and efficiency, so the js-objectDetect library only works with stump cascades that are stored as JSON.

Using js-objectDetect

The library makes it very easy to use the Viola-Jones algorithm, which is extremely powerful, without even needing to install OpenCV (a large C++ framework for computer vision). It is licensed under GPL so you can freely read the code and modify it. It is also well commented, so if you are interested in the implementation details of the Viola-Jones algorithm, then it is definitely a good place to start. In the next chapter we will be using object detection as input but for this chapter, to demonstrate tracking, we will be drawing a rectangle around a face instead. Facial detection is a common use of computer vision because it is the basis of most more advanced computer vision topics, such as facial recognition or eye tracking.

▓ **Note** As with motion detection, tracking is still dependent on the 2D image produced by the webcam, so it may not be completely accurate and does require good lighting and only one face to track.

It is actually extremely easy to use js-objectDetect for facial detection; it just requires the library to be included and a small bit of JavaScript to run it. It does not use canvas, so the getUserMedia can be set up directly with a video element rather than worrying about canvas contexts. The library is of course included in the download that complements this book. I have included a div with the class cursor; this is the box that surrounds the face that has been detected.

```
<!DOCTYPE html>
<html>
<head>
    <title>Webcam Stuff</title>
    <style>
        html, body { margin: 0; padding: 0; }
        video { position: absolute; top: 0; left: 0;  }
    </style>
</head>
<body>
    <video></video>
    <div class="cursor"></div>

    <script src="js-objectDetect/compatibility.js"></script>
    <script src="js-objectDetect/smoother.js"></script>

    <script src="js-objectDetect/objectdetect.js"></script>
    <script src="js-objectDetect/objectdetect.frontalface.js"></script>
```

```html
    <script src="js-objectDetect/jquery.js"></script>
    <script src="js-objectDetect/jquery.objectdetect.js"></script>

    <script src="script.js"></script>
</body>
</html>
```

The JavaScript required (within script.js) is comprised of a set-up function that handles the dimensions of the video element as well as the getUserMedia that calls the draw function to run the detection on each frame. There is also a jQuery function that is used to actually draw the square around the face. This works by getting dimensions from the library and modifies the css of the div to fit it.

```javascript
window.URL = window.URL || window.webkitURL;
navigator.getUserMedia = navigator.getUserMedia ||
                         navigator.webkitGetUserMedia ||
                         navigator.mozGetUserMedia ||
                         navigator.msGetUserMedia;
if (navigator.getUserMedia === undefined) {
    if (console !== undefined) {
        console.log("Browser doesn't support getUserMedia");
    }
}

window.addEventListener('DOMContentLoaded', setup);

function setup()  {
    videoElement = document.querySelector("video");
    videoElement.width = w = window.innerWidth;
    videoElement.height = h = window.innerHeight;
    videoElement.autoplay = true;

    navigator.getUserMedia({video: true}, function (stream) {
        videoElement.src = window.URL.createObjectURL(stream);
        videoElement.addEventListener('canplay', draw);
    }, function() {});
}

$.fn.highlight = function(rect, color) {
    $('.cursor').css({
        "border":   "2px solid " + color,
        "position": "absolute",
        "left":     ($(this).offset().left + rect[0]) + "px",
        "top":      ($(this).offset().top  + rect[1]) + "px",
        "width":    rect[2] + "px",
        "height":   rect[3] + "px",
        "z-index": 2
    });
}
```

```
function draw()  {
    $("video").objectdetect("all", {classifier: objectdetect.frontalface}, function(faces) {
        for (var i = 0; i < faces.length; ++i) {
            $(this).highlight(faces[i], "red");
        }
    });

    requestAnimationFrame(draw);
}
```

Summary

I hope that from this chapter you have gained a deeper understanding of how to manipulate video in real time and use it to produce useful solutions. Motion detection and object tracking are the two key starting points of computer vision. Although there may not currently be many use-cases for computer vision on the web, we are starting to see more and more of it, such as detecting faces in photos to tag people. Some companies (*ahem* Facebook) are going as far as facial recognition, which has its basis in facial detection. Many people consider computer vision to be incredibly complicated, something that only academia need to be interested in, but that's just not the case. I highly recommend you to look further into this topic, much of it is beyond the scope of this book but if you take a look at the appendix you will find some extra information and useful resources for further reading. The next chapter builds on some of the concepts in this chapter, although we will be using a fairly naïve algorithm for detecting the movement of a finger so that we can use it to play a note on the keyboard that we built earlier in the book. Hopefully you can see that either by writing naïve algorithms or using libraries other people have already worked on, it is not as difficult to get started with computer vision as most people think it is and it is even more accessible now that it can be achieved, without relying on C++ or other more difficult languages, using HTML5 and JavaScript!

■ ■ ■

CHAPTER 10

Interacting with the Browser Using Gestures

This chapter aims to take everything you've learned so far and put it all together to make an ambitious music creation web app that allows multiple people to play instruments, using computer-generated audio, at the same time using just JavaScript, Node.js, and some HTML5 APIs. Oh, and it also needs to use the webcam to allow input using your fingers in the air.

As I'm sure you can imagine this is a massive task. This chapter gets you to a basic version of it and allows you to extend the task however you please. For example, instead of tracking all fingers so that you can play the keyboard properly, it will instead have a cursor that you can move left or right by pointing in that direction, or pointing in the middle to simulate a key press.

Taking the Keyboard Server-Side

We base this project on the keyboard from Chapter 5. Currently, the keyboard is set up so that you can play multiple notes at once (which is a good start) but we need to modify it so that multiple people can play multiple notes. Of course, even if two people are playing the same note, it should only be played once. This is ideal as it means we only need one set of oscillators per person, so when person B starts playing a note it will play using the set of oscillators that person A is using.

Previously we turned off the oscillator within stopSound but this can cause issues with race conditions (that is, things done always happen in the order you expect) and since you cannot play a stopped oscillator, it is better to delete it (in this case, we will set it to null) and create a new one (which we were doing anyway). To make it easier to check existence of an oscillator, I've changed the array initialization loops to set the indexes to null instead of creating new oscillators to begin with.

```
// White Keys
var o = new Array(21);
for (var i = 0; i < 21; i++) {
    o[i] = null;
}

// Black Keys
var ob = new Array(15);
for (var i = 0; i < 15; i++) {
    ob[i] = null;
}
```

```
function stopSound(i, black)  {
    var osc;
    if (black) {
        osc = ob[i];
    } else {
        osc = o[i];
    }
    if ((black && ob[i] !== null) || (!black && o[i] !== null)) {
        osc.noteOff(0);
        osc.disconnect();
        if (black) {
        ob[i] = null;
        } else {
        o[i] = null;
        }
    }
}
```

The playSound function now needs to only play a new sound if there is no oscillator already on the key; otherwise it will cause problems such as not being able to stop it playing or it will only play for a short amount of time. I've also cleaned it up a little so that the same conditions are not checked twice without needing to be. Note that I've changed ctx to actx, this is so that it is obviously an Audio Context and to avoid confusion with the Canvas Context used for the computer vision.

```
var gainNode = actx.createGainNode();
gainNode.connect(actx.destination);

function playSound(i, black) {
    if ((black && ob[i] === null) || (!black && o[i] === null)) {
        var osc = actx.createOscillator();
        var freq;
        if (black)  {
            freq = blackNotes[i];
        }
        else  {
            freq = whiteNotes[i];
        }
        osc.type = 3;
        osc.frequency.value = freq;
        osc.connect(gainNode);
        osc.noteOn(0);
        if (black) {
        ob[i] = osc;
        } else {
        o[i] = osc;
        }
    }
}
```

So now the keyboard is set up a little better and we can write the server code. Socket.IO allows you to define the structure of all communication between the client and server in a very nice way; each message is a task that is usually passed on to the other clients. The keyboard has two tasks: play sounds and stop playing sounds. All we need is a couple of listeners for messages that play or stop sounds.

```
socket.on('play_sound', function (data) {
    data.color = socket.color;
    console.log("play sound %j", data);
    socket.broadcast.to(room).emit('play_sound', data);
});

socket.on('stop_sound', function (data) {
    console.log("stop sound %j", data);
    socket.broadcast.to(room).emit('stop_sound', data);
});
```

You may have noticed that we send a color to everyone in the room; this is so that they can easily see keys that other people have pressed. I've not created them uniquely, using a database or anything, but when the socket originally connects it creates a random color. I've done this by creating a random number and multiplying it by 16777215, this is essentially the same as doing a bitwise shift on the hex color for white (#ffffff).

```
socket.color = '#'+ ('000000' + Math.floor(Math.random()*16777215).toString(16)).slice(-6);
```

And that's it! The rest of the server-side code is the same as we had in Chapter 7.

server.js

```
var express = require('express'),
    http = require('http'),
    uuid = require ("node-uuid"),
    app = express(),
    server = http.createServer(app),
    io = require('socket.io').listen(server);
io.set('log level', 1); // Removes debug logs
app.use(express.static('public'));
server.listen(8080);

app.get('/:id', function (req, res) {
    res.sendfile(__dirname + '/index.html');
});

io.sockets.on('connection', function (socket) {

    var room = socket.handshake.headers.referer;
    console.log('JOINED', room);
    socket.join(room);
    socket.id = uuid.v1();
    socket.color = '#'+ ('000000' + Math.floor(Math.random()*16777215).toString(16)).slice(-6);

    io.sockets.in(room).emit('room_count', io.sockets.manager.rooms['/' + room].length);
```

```
    // WebRTC signalling
    socket.on('received_offer', function(data) {
        console.log("received_offer %j", data);
        io.sockets.in(room).emit('received_offer', data);
    });

    socket.on('received_candidate', function(data) {
        console.log("received_candidate %j", data);
        io.sockets.in(room).emit('received_candidate', data);
    });

    socket.on('received_answer', function(data) {
        console.log("received_answer %j", data);
        io.sockets.in(room).emit('received_answer', data);
    });

    // Chatroom messages
    socket.on('message', function (data) {
        io.sockets.in(room).emit('message', data);
    });

    // Music
    socket.on('play_sound', function (data) {
        data.color = socket.color;
        console.log("play sound %j", data);
        socket.broadcast.to(room).emit('play_sound', data);
    });

    socket.on('stop_sound', function (data) {
        console.log("stop sound %j", data);
        socket.broadcast.to(room).emit('stop_sound', data);
    });

    // Close socket and let others know
    socket.on('close', function () {
        console.log("closed %j", room);
        io.sockets.in(room).emit('closed', room);
        socket.leave(room);
    });

});
```

On the client-side we need to both send the messages, as well as handle received messages. To begin with, let's set the color. We set a variable called color when the 'color' message is received (when you break it down bit by bit, this really is simple!).

```
socket.on('color', function(data)  {
    color = data;
})
```

When the play or stop messages are received, we need to call the corresponding function; on play we also need to set the color of the particular key to be the color that relates to the person that sent it. On stop, the colors should go back to being black or white.

```
socket.on('play_sound', function(data) {
    if (data.black) {
        bkeys[data.i].fill({ color: data.color });
    } else {
        keys[data.i].fill({ color: data.color });
    }
    playSound(data.i, data.black);
});

socket.on('stop_sound', function(data) {
    if (data.black) {
        bkeys[data.i].fill({ color: '#000' });
    } else {
        keys[data.i].fill({ color: '#fff' });
    }
    stopSound(data.i, data.black);
});
```

To send the messages, we just emit the i and black variables, as well as the color. These need to be emitted every time a key is pressed—including through mouse, keyboard, and webcam inputs. Note that we don't just emit on playSound or stopSound because they are called when a message is received and this causes a circular loop. With the emmited messages added, the code for all inputs looks like the following:

```
var keys = [];
var cursor = [];
for (var i = 0; i < 21; i++)  {
    keys[i] = keyboard.rect(width/21, height);
    keys[i].move(width/21 * i, 0);
    keys[i].attr({ fill: '#fff', stroke: '#000', id: "key"+i });
    keys[i].mousedown ((function(n) {
        return function()  {
            var key = SVG.get("key"+n);
            key.fill({ color: '#f06' });
            socket.emit('play_sound', { "i":n,"black":false});
            playSound(n, false);
        }
    })(i));

    keys[i].mouseup((function(n)  {
        return function() {
            keys[n].fill({ color: '#fff' });
            socket.emit('stop_sound', { "i":n,"black":false});
            stopSound(n, false);
        }
    })(i));
```

```
        cursor[i] = keyboard.circle(width/21);
        cursor[i].attr({ fill: '#ff0000' });
        cursor[i].move(width/21 * i, height / 1.5);
        cursor[i].hide();
}

var bkeys = [];
var prev = 0;
for (var i = 0; i < 15; i++)  {
    bkeys[i] = keyboard.rect(width/42, height / 1.7);
    bkeys[i].attr({ fill: '#000', stroke: '#000', id: "bkey"+i });
    bkeys[i].move(prev + (width/(21*1.3)), 0);
    prev = prev + width/21;
    if (i == 1 || i == 4 || i == 6 || i == 9 || i == 11)  {
        prev += width/21;
    }

    bkeys[i].mousedown ((function(n) {
        return function()  {
            var key = SVG.get("bkey"+n);
            key.fill({ color: '#f06' });
            socket.emit('play_sound', { "i":n,"black":true});
            playSound(n, true);
        }
    })(i));

    bkeys[i].mouseup((function(n)  {
        return function() {
            bkeys[n].fill({ color: '#000' });
            socket.emit('stop_sound', { "i":n,"black":true});
            stopSound(n, true);
        }
    })(i));
}

window.addEventListener('keypress', function(e) {
    for (var i = 0; i < keyboardPressKeys.length; i++)  {
        if (e.keyCode == keyboardPressKeys[i]) {
            var n = i + octave * 7;
            var key = SVG.get("key"+n);
            key.fill({ color: '#f06' });
            socket.emit('play_sound', { "i":n,"black":false, "color":color});
            playSound(n, false);
        }
    }
    for (var i = 0; i < blackKeyPress.length; i++)  {
        if (e.keyCode == blackKeyPress[i]) {
            var n = i + (octave * 5);
            var key = SVG.get("bkey"+n);
            key.fill({ color: '#f06' });
            socket.emit('play_sound', { "i":n,"black":true, "color":color});
```

```
            playSound(n, true);
        }
    }
    if (e.keyCode == 97 && octave > 0) {
        --octave;
    }
    if (e.keyCode == 108 && octave < 2) {
        ++octave;
    }
});

window.addEventListener('keyup', function(e) {
    console.log(e.keyCode);
    for (var i = 0; i < keyboardKeys.length; i++)  {
        if (e.keyCode == keyboardKeys[i]) {
            var key = SVG.get("key"+(i+octave*7));
            key.fill({ color: '#fff' });
            socket.emit('stop_sound', { "i":i+octave*7,"black":false, "color":color });
            stopSound(i+octave*7, false);
        }
    }
    for (var i = 0; i < blackKeys.length; i++)  {
        if (e.keyCode == blackKeys[i]) {
            var n = i + octave * 5;
            var key = SVG.get("bkey"+n);
            key.fill({ color: '#000' });
            socket.emit('stop_sound', { "i":n,"black":true, "color":color });
            stopSound(n, true);
        }
    }
});
```

So now, every time a key is pressed on the keyboard it plays to everybody in the room. This is a good example of how you can go from something simple such as a chatroom to something far more advanced with minimal actual differences to how it works. Figure 11-1 shows an example of two notes being played, with the keys filled with the colour that is unique to the user.

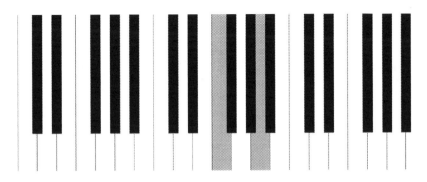

Figure 11-1. *The keyboard playing with keys of the user's own color*

Controlling the Music with a Webcam

Adding motion control to the keyboard is just a matter of implementing the steps from the previous chapter. We start by capturing two frames of the webcam and analyzing it to find motion between the two frames. Remember, we are not using any artificial intelligence to do this so you may need to fiddle with the numbers to make it accurate for your lighting conditions and distance from the screen (as well as movement behind you).

To find the motion, we iterate through the pixels of the second frame comparing them to the previous frame. If they are different, then change the color to black otherwise make it white. For this example we only need motion on the X axis so, every time motion is detected, we add the percentage of the width that corresponds to the X position of the movement. For example, `motionX += 100*(x/w);`. Once everything has been checked, we can divide it by the count to find the average X position. Due to simple math this is not completely accurate, but it is enough to find an indication of motion. Depending on the orientation of the canvas, you may need to invert the numbers to mirror motion correctly: `motionX = 100 - motionX;`.

Now, we can check to see whether `motionX` is within the bounds of the particular motion we are looking for. In this we want to move a cursor left and right, pressing the key if there is motion in the middle third. So if `motionX` is less than 100/3, then move left. If it is between 100/3 and (100/3)*2, then press the key or if it is above (100/3)*2, then move right.

This example only works for the white keys, but you could quite easily extend it to include black keys by finding motion on the Y-axis as well.

```
function motionDetection(data, oldData)  {
    var motionX = 0;
    var count = 0;

    // Iterate through each pixel, changing to 255 if it has not changed
    for( var y = 0 ; y < h; y++ ) {
        for( var x = 0 ; x < w; x++ ) {
            var indexOld = (y * w + x) * 4,
                    oldr = oldData[indexOld],
                    oldg = oldData[indexOld+1],
                    oldb = oldData[indexOld+2],
                    olda = oldData[indexOld+3];
            var indexNew = (y * w + x) * 4,
                    r = data[indexNew],
                    g = data[indexNew+1],
                    b = data[indexNew+2],
                    a = data[indexNew+3];

            if (oldr > r - 30 || oldg > g - 30 || oldb > b - 30)
            {
                data[indexNew] = 255;
                data[indexNew+1] = 255;
                data[indexNew+2] = 255;
                data[indexNew+3] = 255;
            }
            else
            {
                data[indexNew] = 0;
                data[indexNew+1] = 0;
                data[indexNew+2] = 0;
                data[indexNew+3] = 255;
```

```
                motionX += 100*(x/w); // motionX = The percentage of W than X is at
                count++;
            }
        }
    }

    motionX = motionX / count;
    motionX = 100 - motionX;
    if (motionX > 0)  {
        if (motionX > 100/3 && motionX < (100/3)*2)  {
            if (o[i] === null)
                playSound(currentCursor, false);
            console.log('2');
        }
        if (motionX > (100/3)*2)  {
            if (currentCursor + 1 < keys.length)  {
                cursor[currentCursor].hide();
                stopSound(currentCursor, false);
                currentCursor++;
                cursor[currentCursor].show();
            }
            console.log('3');
        }
        if (motionX < 100/3) {
            if (currentCursor - 1 >=0)  {
                cursor[currentCursor].hide();
                stopSound(currentCursor, false);
                currentCursor--;
                cursor[currentCursor].show();
            }
            console.log('1');
        }
    }
    return data;
}
```

The cursor is a round red dot that is created at the same time as the keys; instead of moving a cursor along the keys it hides and only shows the correct one.

```
cursor[i] = keyboard.circle(width/21);
cursor[i].attr({ fill: '#ff0000' });
cursor[i].move(width/21 * i, height / 1.5);
cursor[i].hide();
```

Now, the project should all be working. You can find the complete code below in Listing 11-1 and in the download that is available on the Apress website at www.apress.com/9781430259442 or on my own website at www.shanehudson.net/javascript-creativity.

Listing 11-1. server.js

```
var express = require('express'),
    http = require('http'),
    uuid = require ("node-uuid"),
    app = express(),
    server = http.createServer(app),
    io = require('socket.io').listen(server);
io.set('log level', 1); // Removes debug logs
app.use(express.static('public'));
server.listen(8080);

app.get('/:id', function (req, res) {
    res.sendfile(__dirname + '/index.html');
});

io.sockets.on('connection', function (socket) {

    var room = socket.handshake.headers.referer;
    console.log('JOINED', room);
    socket.join(room);
    socket.id = uuid.v1();
    socket.color = '#'+ ('000000' + Math.floor(Math.random()*16777215).toString(16)).slice(-6);

    io.sockets.in(room).emit('room_count', io.sockets.manager.rooms['/' + room].length);

    // WebRTC signalling
    socket.on('received_offer', function(data) {
        console.log("received_offer %j", data);
        io.sockets.in(room).emit('received_offer', data);
    });

    socket.on('received_candidate', function(data) {
        console.log("received_candidate %j", data);
        io.sockets.in(room).emit('received_candidate', data);
    });

    socket.on('received_answer', function(data) {
        console.log("received_answer %j", data);
        io.sockets.in(room).emit('received_answer', data);
    });

    // Chatroom messages
    socket.on('message', function (data) {
        io.sockets.in(room).emit('message', data);
    });
```

```
    // Music
    socket.on('play_sound', function (data) {
        data.color = socket.color;
        console.log("play sound %j", data);
        socket.broadcast.to(room).emit('play_sound', data);
    });

    socket.on('stop_sound', function (data) {
        console.log("stop sound %j", data);
        socket.broadcast.to(room).emit('stop_sound', data);
    });

    // Close socket and let others know
    socket.on('close', function () {
        console.log("closed %j", room);
        io.sockets.in(room).emit('closed', room);
        socket.leave(room);
    });

});

script.js
var socket = io.connect('http://localhost:8080');
try {
    if (! window.AudioContext) {
        if (window.webkitAudioContext) {
            window.AudioContext = window.webkitAudioContext;
        }
    }

    actx = new AudioContext();
}
catch(e) {
    console.log('Web Audio API is not supported in this browser');
}

window.URL = window.URL || window.webkitURL;
navigator.getUserMedia  =  navigator.getUserMedia ||
                           navigator.webkitGetUserMedia ||
                           navigator.mozGetUserMedia;
if (navigator.getUserMedia === undefined) {
    if (console !== undefined) {
        console.log("Browser doesn't support getUserMedia");
    }
}

var videoElement, canvas, ctx, manip, w, h;
var oldData = null;

window.addEventListener('DOMContentLoaded', setup);
```

```
function setup()  {
    videoElement = document.querySelector("video");
    videoElement.width = w = window.innerWidth;
    videoElement.height = h = window.innerHeight;
    videoElement.autoplay = true;

    canvas = document.createElement('canvas');
    canvas.width = w;
    canvas.height = h;
    ctx = canvas.getContext('2d');

    bcanvas = document.createElement('canvas');
    bcanvas.width = w;
    bcanvas.height = h;
    bctx = bcanvas.getContext('2d');

    navigator.getUserMedia({video: true}, function (stream) {
        videoElement.src = window.URL.createObjectURL(stream);
        videoElement.addEventListener('canplay', draw);
    }, function() {});
}

var width = window.innerWidth;
var height = window.innerHeight;
var keyboard = SVG('keyboard');

var keyboardKeys = [83,68,70,71,72,74,75];
var blackKeys = [69,82,89,85,73];

var keyboardPressKeys = [115,100,102,103,104,106,107];
var blackKeyPress = [101, 114, 121, 117, 105];

var octave = 1; // where octave 1 = middle C

var currentCursor = 10;
var color;

var keys = [];
var cursor = [];
for (var i = 0; i < 21; i++)  {
    keys[i] = keyboard.rect(width/21, height);
    keys[i].move(width/21 * i, 0);
    keys[i].attr({ fill: '#fff', stroke: '#000', id: "key"+i });
    keys[i].mousedown ((function(n) {
        return function()  {
            var key = SVG.get("key"+n);
            key.fill({ color: '#f06' });
            socket.emit('play_sound', { "i":n,"black":false});
            playSound(n, false);
        }
    })(i));
```

```
    keys[i].mouseup((function(n)  {
        return function() {
            keys[n].fill({ color: '#fff' });
            socket.emit('stop_sound', { "i":n,"black":false});
            stopSound(n, false);
        }
    })(i));

    cursor[i] = keyboard.circle(width/21);
    cursor[i].attr({ fill: '#ff0000' });
    cursor[i].move(width/21 * i, height / 1.5);
    cursor[i].hide();
}

var bkeys = [];
var prev = 0;
for (var i = 0; i < 15; i++)  {
    bkeys[i] = keyboard.rect(width/42, height / 1.7);
    bkeys[i].attr({ fill: '#000', stroke: '#000', id: "bkey"+i });
    bkeys[i].move(prev + (width/(21*1.3)), 0);
    prev = prev + width/21;
    if (i == 1 || i == 4 || i == 6 || i == 9 || i == 11)  {
        prev += width/21;
    }

    bkeys[i].mousedown ((function(n) {
        return function()  {
            var key = SVG.get("bkey"+n);
            key.fill({ color: '#f06' });
            socket.emit('play_sound', { "i":n,"black":true});
            playSound(n, true);
        }
    })(i));

    bkeys[i].mouseup((function(n)  {
        return function() {
            bkeys[n].fill({ color: '#000' });
            socket.emit('stop_sound', { "i":n,"black":true});
            stopSound(n, true);
        }
    })(i));
}


window.addEventListener('keypress', function(e) {
    for (var i = 0; i < keyboardPressKeys.length; i++)  {
        if (e.keyCode == keyboardPressKeys[i]) {
            var n = i + octave * 7;
            var key = SVG.get("key"+n);
            key.fill({ color: '#f06' });
            socket.emit('play_sound', { "i":n,"black":false, "color":color});
            playSound(n, false);
```

```
            }
        }
        for (var i = 0; i < blackKeyPress.length; i++) {
            if (e.keyCode == blackKeyPress[i]) {
                var n = i + (octave * 5);
                var key = SVG.get("bkey"+n);
                key.fill({ color: '#f06' });
                socket.emit('play_sound', { "i":n,"black":true, "color":color});
                playSound(n, true);
            }
        }
        if (e.keyCode == 97 && octave > 0) --octave;
        if (e.keyCode == 108 && octave < 2) ++octave;
    });

    window.addEventListener('keyup', function(e) {
        console.log(e.keyCode);
        for (var i = 0; i < keyboardKeys.length; i++) {
            if (e.keyCode == keyboardKeys[i]) {
                var key = SVG.get("key"+(i+octave*7));
                key.fill({ color: '#fff' });
                socket.emit('stop_sound', { "i":i+octave*7,"black":false, "color":color });
                stopSound(i+octave*7, false);
            }
        }
        for (var i = 0; i < blackKeys.length; i++) {
            if (e.keyCode == blackKeys[i]) {
                var n = i + octave * 5;
                var key = SVG.get("bkey"+n);
                key.fill({ color: '#000' });
                socket.emit('stop_sound', { "i":n,"black":true, "color":color });
                stopSound(n, true);
            }
        }
    });

    var gainNode = actx.createGainNode();
    gainNode.connect(actx.destination);

    // White Keys
    var o = new Array(21);
    for (var i = 0; i < 21; i++) {
        o[i] = null;
    }

    // Black Keys
    var ob = new Array(15);
    for (var i = 0; i < 15; i++) {
        ob[i] = null;
    }
```

```
var PI_2 = Math.PI*2;
var SAMPLE_RATE = 44100;

var whiteNotes = [130.82, 146.83, 164.81, 174.61, 196, 220, 246.94, 261.63, 293.66, 329.63, 349.23,
392, 440, 493.88, 523.25, 587.33, 659.26, 698.46, 783.99, 880, 987.77];
var blackNotes = [138.59, 155.56, 185, 207.65, 233.08, 277.18, 311.13, 369.99, 415.3, 466.16,
554.37, 622.25, 739.99, 830.61, 932.33];

function playSound(i, black) {
    if ((black && ob[i] === null) || (!black && o[i] === null)) {
        var osc = actx.createOscillator();
        var freq;
        if (black)  {
            freq = blackNotes[i];
        }
        else  {
            freq = whiteNotes[i];
        }
        osc.type = 3;
        osc.frequency.value = freq;
        osc.connect(gainNode);
        osc.noteOn(0);
        if (black) ob[i] = osc;
        else o[i] = osc;
    }
}

function stopSound(i, black)  {
    var osc;
    if (black) osc = ob[i];
    else osc = o[i];
    if ((black && ob[i] !== null) || (!black && o[i] !== null)) {
        osc.noteOff(0);
        osc.disconnect();
        if (black) ob[i] = null;
        else o[i] = null;
    }
}

socket.on('color', function(data)  {
  color = data;
});

socket.on('play_sound', function(data) {
    if (data.black)
        bkeys[data.i].fill({ color: data.color });
    else
        keys[data.i].fill({ color: data.color });
    playSound(data.i, data.black);
});
```

```
socket.on('stop_sound', function(data) {
    if (data.black)
        bkeys[data.i].fill({ color: '#000' });
    else
        keys[data.i].fill({ color: '#fff' });
    stopSound(data.i, data.black);
});

function draw() {
    if (videoElement.paused || videoElement.ended) {
        return;
    }
    try {
        bctx.drawImage(videoElement, 0, 0, w, h);
        manip = bctx.getImageData(0, 0, w, h);
        var data = manip.data;
        if (oldData != null) {
            data = motionDetection(data, oldData);
            ctx.putImageData(manip, 0, 0);
            oldData = null;
        }
        else {
            oldData = manip.data;
        }

        requestAnimationFrame(draw);
    }
    catch (e) {
        if (e.name == "NS_ERROR_NOT_AVAILABLE") {
            setTimeout(draw, 0);
        }
        else {
            throw e;
        }
    }
}

function motionDetection(data, oldData) {
    var motionX = 0;
    var count = 0;

    // Iterate through each pixel, changing to 255 if it has not changed
    for( var y = 0 ; y < h; y++ ) {
        for( var x = 0 ; x < w; x++ ) {
            var indexOld = (y * w + x) * 4,
                    oldr = oldData[indexOld],
                    oldg = oldData[indexOld+1],
                    oldb = oldData[indexOld+2],
                    olda = oldData[indexOld+3];
            var indexNew = (y * w + x) * 4,
```

```
                     r = data[indexNew],
                     g = data[indexNew+1],
                     b = data[indexNew+2],
                     a = data[indexNew+3];

            if (oldr > r - 30 || oldg > g - 30 || oldb > b - 30)
            {
                data[indexNew] = 255;
                data[indexNew+1] = 255;
                data[indexNew+2] = 255;
                data[indexNew+3] = 255;
            }
            else
            {
                data[indexNew] = 0;
                data[indexNew+1] = 0;
                data[indexNew+2] = 0;
                data[indexNew+3] = 255;

                motionX += 100*(x/w); // motionX = The percentage of W than X is at
                count++;
            }
        }
    }
}

motionX = motionX / count;
motionX = 100 - motionX;
var key = SVG.get("key"+currentCursor);

if (motionX > 0)  {
    if (motionX > 100/3 && motionX < (100/3)*2)  {
        if (o[i] === null)  {
            key.fill({ color: '#f06' });
            playSound(currentCursor, false);
        }
        console.log('2');
    }
    if (motionX > (100/3)*2)  {
        if (currentCursor + 1 < keys.length)  {
            cursor[currentCursor].hide();
            key.fill({ color: '#fff' });
            stopSound(currentCursor, false);
            currentCursor++;
            cursor[currentCursor].show();
        }
        console.log('3');
    }
    if (motionX < 100/3) {
        if (currentCursor - 1 >=0)  {
            cursor[currentCursor].hide();
            key.fill({ color: '#fff' });
            stopSound(currentCursor, false);
```

```
            currentCursor--;
            cursor[currentCursor].show();
        }
        console.log('1');
    }
  }
  return data;
}
```

In Figure 11-2 you can see an example of controlling the cursor (the circle) to press keys on the keyboard using motion detection through a webcam.

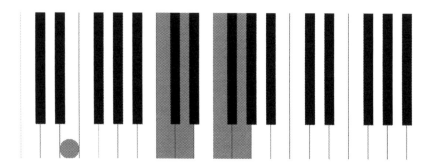

Figure 11-2. *The keyboard controlled using the cursor through the webcam*

Summary

This chapter was mostly about putting it all together, as the previous chapters explained the techniques. I hope it has helped you but also shown you just how easy it is to do some quite impressive things, if you just take it bit by bit. You've gone from making a square slide in canvas to moving your hands to make the browser generate sounds.

There are quite a few ways for you to improve the project, such as making the webcam work with black keys (you could perhaps do this by looking for motion on the Y axis as well as the X axis). Or you can just go ahead and make something else—but remember you learn the most by playing around with the code, not just reading a book. I hope you've enjoying reading this book. The appendix provides some extra information that is considered out of the scope of the main bulk of the book, as well as recommendations for further reading.

CHAPTER 11

■ ■ ■

Appendix

It was difficult to narrow down content for this book, with a title like *JavaScript Creativity* it could have gone on forever! So this appendix is going to be fairly unstructured, with a few random tidbits that I wanted to mention but couldn't put within the main bulk of the book.

The Future

We are at a very good point on the web, we no longer have to cope with many of the limitations that we've been used to over the years (ancient browsers, dial-up, etc.) but more importantly we have access to more than before. Browsers don't just have better CSS; they now have features such as local storage and device APIs. We made heavy use of the Web Audio API and WebRTC in this book, but there are so many others. The laptop I am writing this on (a Macbook Pro) has an accelerometer that I can read using JavaScript. It may not be the most useful thing ever, but somebody might find a clever use for it (measuring the G-force of the train that I'm writing this on, perhaps?).

I named this book *JavaScript Creativity* not because you can make pretty things in canvas (although that is still an incredible feature to have), but instead because of the creative ways you can use web technologies these days. A webcam-controlled piano that generates notes on the fly? It is by no means perfect, but we've done that! A website that uses GPS to give you relevant news about the area you're in? Absolutely doable. In Chapter 2 we produced line-art from a photo and turned that into a coloring book app–these things just were not possible even a few years ago.

There are a lot of features that are being added to the web (or at least being written about in specifications) that don't have obvious use cases. Of course every feature is proposed for a reason, but some of the features (such as Device Proximity) could be used for a number of interesting non-obvious uses. And that is very good, that is "JavaScript Creativity". In fact, I've seen robots that can navigate buildings, avoiding objects and even some that can fly–all written using JavaScript.

The key to creating future technology is–and always has been–to ask "what if" questions. What if I could control a keyboard with my fingers? What if a news website knew my location? Not everything has an obvious answer, and I've even argued in the past that not everything should be made. But it is always worth considering circumstances and ideas, even if they seem outlandish at first.

Further Reading

While I was writing this book, I came across quite a few incredibly interesting articles and books that you may be interested in. They are not all directly related to the chapters in this book but they may worth reading anyway. Some are very technical, such as the intricacies of JavaScript or a particular algorithm, whilst others are more conceptual. As I've said throughout the book, you should not learn how to make a particular project but instead how to use the techniques in a variety of situations, so the conceptual and high-level articles (although not directly within the scope of this book) are worth reading. I will keep a more up-to-date list on my website at `www.shanehudson.net/javascript-creativity/`, as well as other resources for the book.

Algorithms

There are a number of algorithms mentioned throughout the book, as well as many others that are worth reading about if you are interested in the more theoretical side of things. More often than not, you can use prewritten algorithms, such as the js-objectdetect library we used in Chapter 9, but a lot of you will probably (like I do) have a hunger to learn the ins and outs of what you are working with. As algorithms are mostly published in academic journals, they may not be easily accessed online but there are usually articles online that do explain the algorithms (often written for lectures at universities). I will give a brief overview of a few algorithms that I recommend you learn more about, but I will avoid touching on the mathematical aspects.

In Chapter 2, we used a naïve edge detection algorithm to convert photos to line art. We did this by averaging the neighbors of each pixel and comparing them to a threshold. As I'm sure you can imagine, this is very inefficient. The final outcome was good enough, but far from perfect. In the chapter I mentioned that there is a better way using Canny Edge Detection, which was developed in 1986 by John F. Canny. It is a five-step algorithm. The first step is to apply a Gaussian filter, a form of blur, to smooth out the edges so that there is less noise; for example, this would smooth the grain of wood on a table so that it can more easily detect the edges of the table. The second step is to find gradients. These are found using the Sobel operator that helps you find both the magnitude and direction of the gradients. The next step is known as "Non-maximum suppression," which essentially means converting blurred edges into sharp edges; this is basically done by removing all low values of gradients. The fourth step uses thresholds. We used thresholds in our naïve algorithm for edge detection; they are useful for lowering the chance of noise. The difference between our version and Canny is that his uses two, called double thresholding, so that both very high values and very low values count as edges but any values in the middle are likely to be noise. This makes it more accurate to find edges that are not obvious. Lastly, to rule out as much noise as possible, weak edges are only counted if they are attached to strong edges.

While I'm talking about algorithms, I would like to quickly remind you about the Fast Fourier Transform (FFT) that we used in Chapter 3 through the Web Audio API. You don't need to implement it, as FFT is a part of the Web Audio API specification, so I won't go into detail (besides, it is heavily math intensive) but it is worth remembering and some of you may be keen to delve further into Fourier transforms. Essentially these transforms, when used with audio (there are many other applications), are used to retrieve frequency data based on a snippet of audio. We used it for visualization of audio, but that is barely scratching the surface of what you can do with direct access to such raw data.

The final algorithm that was mentioned in the chapters was the Viola-Jones object recognition framework (it is classed as a framework because the original paper did not describe an implementation for the algorithm, just the components that are required), in explaining that I also briefly described Haar-like features. I will not go into further explanation here, but do look further into Viola-Jones and perhaps even try writing your own implementation of it.

Links

Throughout the book I've linked to various resources, I've collected these here so that they are easy to find.

- www.apress.com/9781430259442–This is the official Apress page for the book. The source code is available here as a download.

- www.shanehudson.net/javascript-creativity–This is my own page for the book. I will try to keep it up to date as a resource to go alongside the book. The source code is available here too.

Chapter 1

- www.html5please.com–HTML5 Please gives useful advice on whether a feature should be used in production, or if there are available polyfills.

- www.caniuse.com–Can I Use gives direct access to the data of browser support down to browser versions and inconstancies between the implementation and the specification.

Chapter 3

- `www.incompetech.com/music/royalty-free`—Imcompetech has a good selection of royalty-free music.

Chapter 4

- `mrdoob.github.io/three.js/`—Three.js is a widely used wrapper for WebGL, which is used for 3D on the web.

- `typeface.neocracy.org`—Here you can find the Helvetiker font that is used as the default font by Three.js.

Chapter 5

- `www.svgjs.com`—This is a lightweight SVG library, which we used in Chapter 5 to handle creating the timeline in the music player.

- `github.com/mattdiamond/Recorderjs`—Matt Diamond's Recorder.js is a script that uses Web Workers to allow recording of Web Audio API nodes.

Chapter 6

- `www.acko.net`—Steven Wittens' site is a masterpiece in its own right, full of incredible articles on mathematics and graphics on the web.

- `www.acko.net/blog/js1k-demo-the-making-of`—This particular article of Steven's was used as the basis of Chapter 6 and I highly recommend you read it.

Chapter 7

- `www.nodejs.org`—This is the official site for Node.js, which is the language used for all server-side code throughout the book.

- `www.github.com/creationix/nvm`—Node Version Manager (NVM) is recommended for handling multiple versions of Node.js.

- `www.nodejs.org/api/index.html`—This is the Node.js documentation, which can be also found from the front page of the main Node.js site.

Chapter 8

- `www.ietf.org/rfc/rfc5245.txt`—RFC 5245 goes into a lot of detail about Interactive Connectivity Establishment (ICE). It is a heavy read, but very useful when dealing with WebRTC.

Chapter 9

- `www.github.com/mtschirs/js-objectdetect`—This library, written by Martin Tschirsich, is a JavaScript implementation based on the Viola-Jones algorithm. It makes it easy to do object detection without getting bogged down with implementation details.

Index

Get the eBook for only $10!

Now you can take the weightless companion with you anywhere, anytime. Your purchase of this book entitles you to 3 electronic versions for only $10.

This Apress title will prove so indispensible that you'll want to carry it with you everywhere, which is why we are offering the eBook in 3 formats for only $10 if you have already purchased the print book.

Convenient and fully searchable, the PDF version enables you to easily find and copy code—or perform examples by quickly toggling between instructions and applications. The MOBI format is ideal for your Kindle, while the ePUB can be utilized on a variety of mobile devices.

Go to www.apress.com/promo/tendollars to purchase your companion eBook.

Apress®
THE EXPERT'S VOICE™